Glues, Brews, and Goos

Glues, Brews, and Goos

Recipes and Formulas for Almost Any Classroom Project

DIANA F. MARKS

Illustrated by
Donna L. Farrell

1996
TEACHER IDEAS PRESS
A Division of
Libraries Unlimited, Inc.
Englewood, Colorado

Dedicated to Peter, Kevin, and Colin,
my obliging sages and supports.

TEACHER IDEAS PRESS
A Division of Libraries Unlimited, Inc.
P.O. Box 6633
Englewood, CO 80155-6633
1-800-237-6124

Production Editor: Jason Cook
Copy Editor: Ramona Gault
Layout and Interior Design: Kay Minnis

Library of Congress Cataloging-in-Publication Data

Marks, Diana F.
  Glues, brews, and goos : recipes and formulas for almost any classroom project / Diana F. Marks ; illustrated by Donna L. Farrell.
    xvi, 179 p. 22x28 cm.
    Includes bibliographical references (p. 177).
    ISBN 1-56308-362-0
    1. Activity programs in education--Handbooks, manuals, etc. I. Title.
  LB1027.25.M26   1996
  372.5--dc20   95-38995
                                                        CIP

Contents

Acknowledgments

I wish to thank my parents, Earl and Shirley Heuchemer, because they have always loved my writing, unconditionally. I wish to thank Donna Farrell, not only for her illustrations, but for her confidence in me. I wish to thank Nita Sides for her concern and understanding. I wish to thank Beth Auwarter for her library expertise and her unflagging optimism. I wish to thank Carol Schmauk for her willingness to try my ideas.

Finally, I wish to thank my students at Wrightstown Elementary School. They always keep me on my toes, and they always have suggestions.

Introduction

Though filled with recipes and formulas, this book really emphasizes children and learning. Students want to do and test and try. They enjoy digging in and examining the results. They learn best when they experience the process. For example, instead of having your students read about volcanoes, have them make a model of one and then create various kinds of volcanic actions. Or, instead of simply discussing the difficulties of living during the 1800s, have students participate in a series of workstations—churning butter, dipping candles, frying journey cakes, assembling pomanders, and fabricating rag paper.

One of the purposes of this book is to connect students to the past. In some cases, this means a distant past. Paper making and batik are ancient crafts. Native Americans dyed clothing and other items using the same processes described in this book. Some entire chapters, such as "Soaps" and "Candles," hark back to long before the Colonial period in America. Apple butter and sourdough bread were favorite pioneer foods. People have been constructing gingerbread houses for many years. Children who grew up after the 1929 stock market crash grew "Depression plants," or charcoal gardens. The past can mean just a few years, as children learn to tie-dye fabric. This book even shows how to age paper so that students can make "pirate maps" or imitations of Civil War diaries.

Another goal is to link students to nature. Adults can help students make bird feeders with recycled materials. Then students can fill these feeders with foods to tempt ornithological taste buds. Students can replicate dinosaur footprints and bird eggs by making plaster of Paris casts. Students can make new wrapping paper from old catalogs. They can turn blueberries into muffins or dyes. They can transform ordinary classroom windows into scenes from a rain forest by using paints specified in this book. Students can see how stalactites and stalagmites grow by making crystal models. They can dry flowers and herbs to make potpourri. Students can demonstrate their knowledge of world geography by making various types of salt maps. They can make and then eat edible examples of such land features as buttes, deltas, and atolls—out of mashed potatoes.

A third objective is to help students see the importance of science to everyday life. For example, when students make some of the paints specified in this book, they will see how pigment is actually the application of chemistry to art. Invisible inks, bubble solutions, and crystals are easy to make and easy to explain. Students can change milk into cheese, grapes into raisins, and bread into clay. Even more, they can combine flour, yeast, and a few other essential ingredients, add some heat, and create breads. They can make an egg bounce and determine whether potatoes contain starch. Students are absolutely fascinated when they mix white glue and liquid starch—the resulting goop bounces, snaps, and crackles!

Another hope of mine is to have students see themselves as part of a global community. Many of the recipes and formulas in this book, from cooking latkes to making piñatas, have multicultural aspects. They can bake soda bread to celebrate Saint Patrick's Day, or make tortillas to honor Cinco de Mayo, or eat challah to mark Rosh Hashanah. Students can create maracas and then spatter-paint them. They can produce a fresco, Diego Rivera style. They can compose a mosaic that the people of Pompeii would have admired, and then make pizza muffins just for the fun of it. They can finish a lesson regarding Scotland by eating scones.

Because students enjoy eating, many of the recipes focus on food. Students can follow the steps of yogurt making and enjoy the final product. Students can make and eat an excellent marzipan teddy bear, peanut brittle, soft pretzels, or fortune cookies. They can top their scratch muffins with homemade peanut butter. They can make fruit leather in September, snickerdoodles in January, caramel corn in February, and water ice in June.

Many of the recipes and formulas have been around for years or even centuries. Others have been updated to include microwave ovens or recycled materials. Some are pure inventions of the author. All the projects have been kid-tested. Most of the materials are easy to obtain, and the directions are simple and clear and designed for students.

Here, at your fingertips, is a treasure chest of recipes and formulas for almost any classroom project. My hope is that this book will be well-thumbed and much used.

Tips

- Always test a formula before using it with students.

- Check to make sure all materials are gathered together before beginning a process.

- Make safety the top priority. Try to anticipate any possible problems and eliminate all dangers. Review safety procedures with students.

- Keep pots, spoons, and utensils used for making food separate from those used in non-food projects.

- Recipes and formulas note when a stove or heating element is required. However, electric frying pans and pots, if available, are preferable. Temperature can be controlled more accurately on electric appliances, and they can be used right in the classroom. Also, the pots and frying pans can be easily transported to a sink for cleaning.

- Because hot running water is not available in many classrooms, cleaning up can be difficult. If running water is not available, use plastic bags to hold ingredients instead of mixing bowls. Students like to seal the bags and mix the contents by squeezing. Though plastic bags are not the most environmentally preferred material, their use may make the difference between carrying out a project or dismissing it as too cumbersome.

- Keep notes on what works and what does not work with your students.

- Experiment and enjoy!

1
Clays and Doughs

Clays and doughs can be divided into two groups, those that dry and those that do not dry. A clay or dough that dries will retain its shape and can be used for permanent projects (e.g., artwork, gifts). A clay or dough that does not dry may not keep its shape if disturbed, so it should only be used for temporary projects (e.g., a primary-age student could use "silly stuff" to form letters of the alphabet).

The following clays and doughs do not need to be fired in a kiln. Clay and dough can clog drains, so never use a sink to dispose of such material.

■ Pearly Clay

[Makes 1-1/2 cups—enough for 1 student]

This clay is very translucent when soft and fairly translucent when dry. It stores well in an airtight container. It will harden within 24 hours.

Materials

1/2 cup salt	stove or heating element
1/2 cup boiling water	pot
1/4 cup cold water	mixing bowl
1/2 cup cornstarch	mixing spoon

Procedure

1. Pour the salt into the boiling water.
2. In a mixing bowl, combine the cornstarch and the cold water.
3. Add the cornstarch mixture to the salt solution.
4. Cook over low heat, stirring constantly.
5. When the mixture is the consistency of stiff cookie dough, remove from heat and let cool.
6. Knead until the clay is pliable.
7. Mold into desired shapes.
8. Let the clay shapes dry overnight, or bake them at 200° for 1 hour.

■ Alum Dough
[Makes 2-1/2 cups—enough for 2 students]

This recipe may be the perfect dough. It keeps without refrigeration for a couple of months, it dries overnight, and it does not have to be cooked.

Materials

3 teaspoons alum
1-1/2 cups flour
1 cup salt
1 cup boiling water
2 teaspoons vegetable oil

mixing bowl
mixing spoon
powdered tempera paints
mixing containers
airtight storage containers

Procedure

1. Combine the dry ingredients in the mixing bowl.
2. Add the boiling water and the oil. Mix thoroughly.
3. Divide the dough into several portions, place in mixing containers, and add tempera paints to achieve desired colors.
4. Model and let dry.
5. Store unused dough in airtight containers.

■ Silly Stuff
[Makes 2-1/4 cups—enough for 2 students]

Similar to commercially prepared doughs, silly stuff is for temporary use. It does not dry well.

Materials

1 cup flour
1/2 cup salt
2 tablespoons vegetable oil
1 cup water
2 teaspoons cream of tartar

food coloring (optional)
stove or heating element
pot
mixing spoon
airtight storage container

Procedure

1. Mix all ingredients in the pot.
2. Cook over medium heat, stirring until the mixture sticks together in a ball.
3. Remove the pot from heat and let the dough cool.
4. Squeeze and knead. Have fun!
5. Store in an airtight container.

■ Bread Slice Clay
[Allow 1 or 2 slices of bread per student]

Bread slice clay has few ingredients. This clay is easy to use with an entire class. Keep lots of paper towels at hand to wipe hands. The clay will keep for a few days.

Materials

1 slice white bread
1 teaspoon white glue
1 teaspoon water

food coloring
acrylic gloss and brush

Procedure

1. Cut off the bread crust.
2. Pour the glue and water into the center of the bread.
3. Knead until it forms a ball (approximately 5 minutes).
4. Add food coloring, if desired.
5. Sculpt the clay and let it harden overnight.
6. Apply acrylic gloss over the piece if you wish to save it for a long time.

■ Soap Clay
[Makes 1-1/4 cups—enough for 1 student]

A shiny product, soap clay can be applied to other surfaces to make "snow."

Materials

3/4 cup powdered laundry soap
1 teaspoon warm water
mixing bowl

mixing spoon
electric mixer

Procedure

1. Mix the soap powder and water in the bowl.
2. Beat with the mixer until it feels like clay.
3. Sculpt the clay. It dries to a shiny finish.

■ Quick Clay
[Makes 2 cups—enough for 2 students]

As the name implies, this clay hardens quickly. It can be stored in a closed container for one month.

Materials

1 cup baking soda
1/2 cup cornstarch
2/3 cup warm water
stove or heating element

pot
mixing spoon
food coloring
acrylic gloss and brush

Procedure

1. Stir together the soda and cornstarch in the pot.
2. Add the water and stir. Heat on medium until it boils. It will look like mashed potatoes.
3. Remove from the stove and let it cool.
4. Knead the clay and add food coloring.
5. Shape the object; let it dry.
6. Finish with acrylic gloss.

■ Flour Clay
[Makes 6 cups enough for 3 students]

Flour clay requires no cooking. It is a versatile clay that can be baked or allowed to air dry. Students can make thin coils of the clay and intertwine them to make baskets. They can also make "bagels" and other bread look-alikes. Flour clay projects last for years and can be painted after the clay has dried.

Materials

4 cups flour
1-1/2 cups warm water
1 cup salt
mixing bowl

mixing spoon
cookie sheet
refrigerator

Procedure

1. Mix the flour, water, and salt and refrigerate for 30 minutes.
2. Make relatively thin baskets, decorations, or other projects.
3. Place on a cookie sheet. Air dry for several days or bake at 300° for 1 hour.
4. Refrigerate any unused clay in a plastic bag.

■ "Salad Dressing" Dough
[Makes 5 cups—enough for 3 students]

This dough is oily, so keep lots of paper towels at hand. It is smooth and fun to work with. It does not dry well, so students should take advantage of this dough's temporary nature and just play.

Materials

1 cup salt
3 cups flour
1 cup water
1/3 cup vegetable oil

3 tablespoons vinegar
mixing bowl
mixing spoon
airtight storage container

Procedure

1. Combine all the ingredients in the mixing bowl.
2. Knead and sculpt.
3. Store leftovers in the airtight container.

■ Coffee Grounds Clay
[Makes 3 cups—enough for 2 students]

Coffee grounds clay will not dry hard. Though it looks like an ordinary clay, it will crumble if manipulated too much. It makes nice (but temporary) coffee grounds castles.

Materials

1 cup dry coffee grounds
   (fresh or used)
1 cup cornmeal
1/4 cup salt

water
mixing bowl
mixing spoon

Procedure

1. Combine the dry ingredients.
2. Add enough water to make a dough.
3. Model the clay.

■ Glue-Shampoo Dough

[Makes 2 cups—enough for 2 students]

This dough requires no cooking. Ingredients are easy to obtain. It coils nicely to make pots, and it can be air dried.

Materials

1/2 cup white glue
1/3 cup shampoo
1-1/2 cups flour

mixing bowl
mixing spoon
paints and paintbrushes (optional)

Procedure

1. Combine all the ingredients in the mixing bowl.
2. Knead in the bowl.
3. Model the dough. Let objects dry for 1 or 2 days.
4. Paint objects, if desired.

■ Cornmeal Dough

[Makes 2-1/2 cups—enough for 2 students]

Grainy and gooey, this dough will air dry to a hard finish. It does not require cooking.

Materials

1 cup cornmeal
1 cup flour
2/3 cup salt
1 cup water

mixing bowl
mixing spoon
airtight storage container

Procedure

1. Combine the dry ingredients in the mixing bowl.
2. Add enough water to make a dough.
3. Allow finished projects to air dry.
4. Store any unused dough in the airtight container.

■ Cornstarch-Glue Dough

[Makes 3-1/4 cups—enough for 3 students]

Easy to make, this dough is white and pliable. It does not dry well.

Materials

1 cup cornstarch
1/2 cup white glue
3/4 cup flour

1 cup water
mixing bowl
mixing spoon

Procedure

1. Combine the cornstarch, glue, and flour in the mixing bowl.
2. Gradually add water and knead.
3. Have fun. This dough should be used the same day it is made.

■ Soap Dough

[Makes 3-1/4 cups dough—enough for 3 students]

The color is part of the dough. It has a slightly slippery feel and does not dry well.

Materials

1/2 cup salt
2 cups flour
1 tablespoon powdered tempera
   paint

1 tablespoon liquid soap
1 cup water
mixing bowl
mixing spoon

Procedure

1. Combine the salt, flour, and tempera paint in the mixing bowl.
2. Stir in the liquid soap.
3. Slowly add water to make a soft dough.
4. Create!

■ Sand Clay
[Makes 2-1/2 cups—enough for 2 students]

When dry, this clay resembles rock—hard and grainy.

Materials

1-1/2 cups sand
1 teaspoon alum
1/2 cup cornstarch
3/4 cup boiling water
powdered tempera paint
   (optional)

stove or heating element
pot
mixing spoon

Procedure

1. Combine the sand, alum, and cornstarch in the pot.
2. Add the boiling water and powdered tempera paint.
3. Heat at medium temperature until it thickens.
4. Cool and model.
5. Air dry for several days.

■ Tissue Paper Bead Clay
[Makes 1-3/4 cups—enough for 2 students]

The tissue paper gives the beads a delicate look. The clay is easy to work with, and the beads can be strung and attached to book marks. Water causes the tissue paper dyes to run; therefore, use only one color of tissue paper in each batch.

Materials

1-1/2 cups shredded tissue paper
1 cup boiling water
1/2 cup flour
mixing bowl

mixing spoon
kneading surface
plastic straws
paints and paintbrushes

Procedure

1. Combine the tissue paper and boiling water. Let stand for several hours.
2. Drain off the water.
3. Stir in the flour bit by bit and knead the clay.
4. Mold the clay around the straws to make beads.
5. Let the beads dry.
6. Remove the straws and paint the beads.

■ Oat Dough
[Makes 3-1/2 cups—enough for 3 students]

The oats give this dough a rough texture. It does not dry well. Use this dough the same day it is made.

Materials

2 cups water	pot
1 cup oatmeal	mixing bowl
1 cup flour	mixing spoon
stove or heating element	cinnamon (optional)

Procedure

1. Heat the water until boiling.
2. Combine the boiling water and oatmeal in the mixing bowl.
3. Add enough flour to make a dough.
4. Add cinnamon for a wonderful smell.
5. Shape and reshape the dough (e.g., students could first model a mountain ridge, then reshape the dough into a plateau, then reshape the dough into a river delta.)

2

Salt Map Mixtures

■ Salt Map Mixture 1
[Makes 2-1/2 cups—enough for 1 map]

This mixture is not as grainy as Salt Map Mixtures 3 and 4. It can be shaped and reshaped while still damp. This mixture is preferable for maps that are to be used on a short-term basis because the dried shapes may crumble over a long period of time.

Materials

1 cup salt	mixing spoon
1 cup flour	wood or cardboard base
1 cup water	paints and paintbrushes
mixing bowl	

Procedure

1. Mix the salt and flour in the bowl. Add enough water to make a soft dough.
2. Apply the mixture to the base in layers. Allow several hours drying time before adding each successive layer.
3. Build up higher elevations by applying new layers.
4. Paint when the map is thoroughly dry (1 to 3 days).

■ Salt Map Mixture 2
[Makes 3-1/2 cups—enough for 1 map]

The alum makes this mixture dry faster than other mixtures in this chapter. The dough is not grainy and can be rolled to make coils. The coils can then be wound to resemble mountains. Edges can be smoothed out. The mountains are hollow, and they dry quickly. Paints can be added during the mixing instead of after the map has dried.

Materials

1 cup salt	mixing bowl
2 cups flour	mixing spoon
2 teaspoons alum	wood or cardboard base
1 cup water	paints and paintbrushes

Procedure

1. Mix the salt, flour, and alum together in the bowl.
2. Add enough water to make a stiff dough.
3. Form into coils.
4. Apply to the wood or cardboard base.
5. Smooth out coils to resemble mountains, river banks, or other features.
6. Paint when thoroughly dry (drying takes 1 day).

■ Salt Map Mixture 3
[Makes 3-1/2 cups—enough for 2 maps]

This grainy, white mixture resembles the rough texture of earth. Because it is quite durable, it should be used on any maps that will be kept for long periods of time.

Materials

2 cups salt
1 cup flour
1-1/2 cups water
mixing bowl

mixing spoon
wood or cardboard base
paints and paintbrushes

Procedure

1. Mix the salt and flour together in the bowl.
2. Add enough water to make a stiff dough.
3. Apply immediately to the wood or cardboard base.
4. Paint when thoroughly dry (1 to 2 days).

■ Salt Map Mixture 4
[Makes 3-1/2 cups—enough for 2 maps]

This formula has a lumpy texture, similar to that of the earth's surface. Therefore, maps made from this recipe look terrific. However, the mixture takes longer to dry than other recipes.

Materials

1-1/2 cups coarse salt, such as that
    found on soft pretzels
1 cup flour
1-1/2 cups water

mixing bowl
mixing spoon
wood or cardboard base
paints and paintbrushes

Procedure

1. Mix the coarse salt and flour together in the bowl.
2. Add enough water to make a stiff dough.
3. Apply immediately to the wood or cardboard base.
4. Paint when thoroughly dry (2 to 3 days).

3
Papier-Mâché

The term *papier-mâché* means "chewed paper." Its origin dates back to ancient China. The French popularized this moldable "pulp" in Europe during the 1600s. Materials are inexpensive and easy to obtain.

Papier-mâché can clog drains. Drain the water from any remaining papier-mâché and toss the unused pulp into a waste basket.

■ Papier-Mâché Pulp
[Makes 1 quart pulp—enough for 3 students]

Papier-mâché pulp resembles clay in texture. It can be stored in a plastic bag for a few days. However, even with the preservative, it eventually can become rank.

Materials

16 pages of newspaper	2 tablespoons papier-mâché paste
water	(see chapter 5)
2 tablespoons ground chalk	bucket
or spackle	blender
2 tablespoons white glue	stove or heating element
1 tablespoon linseed oil	large cooking pot
2 drops oil of cloves or oil of	sieve
wintergreen, to prevent spoilage*	mixing bowl

*Oil of cloves and oil of wintergreen are toxic. Use them with care. If you plan to use the pulp within a day or two, omit the oils. These oils can be purchased from chemical supply houses or health food stores.

Procedure

1. Tear the newspaper into 1-inch square pieces.
2. Put the pieces into the bucket. Cover with water and soak overnight.
3. The following day, drain most of the water from the bucket. Move the paper to a large pot with 1/2 gallon of water and boil for 20 minutes.
4. Use the blender to make the paper into a pulp.
5. Strain the pulp through the sieve to get out extra water.
6. Form a ball out of the pulp and squeeze more water (but not all of the water) from the pulp.
7. Transfer the pulp to a mixing bowl. Add the rest of the ingredients and mix.
8. The pulp can now be molded, sculpted, carved, and so on. When it is dry, it can be sanded and painted.

■ Molding with Papier-Mâché

Papier-mâché strips should be layered over an existing model. When the papier-mâché dries, the original mold is removed. Plastic bowls and boxes make the best molds because they will neither break nor absorb moisture from the papier-mâché.

Materials

mold (bowl, box, etc.)
petroleum jelly
newspaper
container filled with water

papier-mâché paste (see chapter 5)
white glue or gesso (to use as a
   sealer) and paintbrush
paints and paintbrushes

Procedure

1. Cover your work area with newspaper.
2. Apply a coating of petroleum jelly all over the mold, so that it can be removed when the project is done. Remember to cover the lip or edges.
3. Rip the newspaper into strips.
4. Dip the first layer only into plain water.
5. Get rid of excess water and place the strips on the mold. Completely cover the mold. Allow it to dry.
6. For all subsequent layers, dip each strip of paper into the papier-mâché paste before applying it to the previous layer.
7. Allow each layer to dry before you add the next layer.
8. After the layers are complete and dry, remove the mold.
9. Seal with white glue or gesso.
10. When the sealer is dry, paint.

■ Very Soft Papier-Mâché

This soft papier-mâché allows you to do fine work, such as facial features, on big papier-mâché pieces. It is great for Halloween projects.

Materials

paper towels, napkins, tissues, or toilet paper
white glue

Procedure

1. Wad tissues and dip them into the white glue.
2. Make into desired shapes.

■ Papier-Mâché Maracas

Here students have a chance to link art and music. The patterns they paint on their maracas are most interesting.

Materials

cardboard tubes from rolls of toilet paper or paper towels
scissors
small balloons
masking tape

newspaper
papier-mâché paste (see chapter 5)
large, dry lima beans
paints and paintbrushes
acrylic gloss and brush (optional)

Procedure

1. Cover your work area with newspaper.
2. Cut the cardboard tubes into 3-inch lengths.
3. Blow up the balloons to the size of large lemons. Tie the ends.
4. Tape each balloon to a length of cardboard tube. This is the frame of the maraca.
5. Cut the newspaper into small strips (6 inches by 2 inches).
6. Dip the newspaper into the papier-mâché paste, and apply to the form of the maraca.
7. Cover the entire form of the maraca, except the very tip of the balloon.
8. Let dry and apply a second coat of newspaper and papier-mâché paste.
9. Let the second layer dry.
10. Pop the balloon. Insert several dry lima beans.
11. Cover the hole with newspaper and papier-mâché paste layers. Let dry.
12. Paint and seal with acrylic gloss, if desired.

■ Making Large Papier-Mâché Objects

One advantage that papier-mâché has over clay is that the former can be used to make large but light-weight items. Students can make just about anything they can imagine using papier-mâché.

Materials

full sheets and strips of newspaper
coat-hanger wire (or chicken wire
   for very large objects)
papier-mâché paste (see chapter 5)

masking tape
white glue and a paintbrush
paints and paintbrushes

Procedure

1. Cover the work area with newspaper.
2. Make a frame for the object by forming wadded newspaper sheets into the approximate size and shape of the desired object.
3. Add wire to the frame to help retain its shape.
4. Wrap masking tape around the wire and newspaper balls.
5. Paint the shape with papier-mâché paste.
6. Cover with strips of newspaper. Make sure that all masking tape is covered with newspaper strips. Allow it to dry.
7. Apply a second coat of papier-mâché paste. Cover again with small pieces of newspaper and allow it to dry.
8. Seal with white glue and let it dry.
9. Paint the object.

■ Papier-Mâché Piñata

A piñata is a good finale to a study of Mexico. Note that it takes more than one week to make.

Materials

balloon
string
newspaper
papier-mâché paste (see chapter 5)
white glue

paints and paintbrushes
feathers, glitter, and other decorative materials
small pieces of candy and small toys for piñata "stuffing"

Procedure

1. Blow up the balloon and knot it. Tie a piece of string around the knot.
2. Rip the newspaper into 3-inch squares.
3. Dip a piece of newspaper into the paste and apply it to the balloon.
4. Repeat step 3 until the balloon is entirely covered—except for a small area near the knot of the balloon, which will serve as an opening for stuffing the piñata (leave the opening large enough to accommodate the candy and toys).
5. Hang the balloon (e.g., in a doorway) overnight.
6. Apply a second layer of newspaper squares the next day, and let dry overnight.
7. Repeat the process until six layers have been applied. Let the project dry.
8. Pop the balloon and remove it.
9. Fill the cavity with the candy and toys.
10. Put one or more layers of papier-mâché over the hole. Let dry.
11. Make several holes for a string to hang the piñata when done.
12. Seal with white glue.
13. After the glue is dry, paint and decorate the piñata.

■ Papier-Mâché Dough

[Makes 4 cups—enough for 3 students]

Ordinarily, papier-mâché is applied to other surfaces (e.g., balloons or wire frames). In this recipe, the papier-mâché dough itself can be shaped into small objects.

Materials

water	newspaper
1 cup flour	bucket
1/2 cup salt	blender
oil of cinnamon or oil of cloves to prevent spoilage*	paints and paintbrushes

*Oil of cinnamon and oil of cloves are toxic. Use with care. If you plan to use the pulp within a day or two, omit the oil. These oils can be purchased from chemical supply houses or health food stores.

Procedure

1. Tear the newspaper into 1-inch squares. Place in the bucket.
2. Cover with water and soak until the next day.
3. Place 1 cup soaked paper and water into the blender. Blend until the paper becomes a pulp.
4. Strain out water and place the pulp into the mixing bowl. Continue with the remaining newspaper until 3 cups of pulp are produced.
5. Combine pulp with flour, salt, and oil of cinnamon or oil of cloves to form a dough.
6. Form any small object. An object with more bulk than a grapefruit should be made using a frame of newspaper, wire, and masking tape (see "Making Large Papier-Mâché Objects," p. 18).
7. Let dry and paint.

4
Plaster of Paris

Plaster of Paris may be hazardous to health if used extensively without protection. The dust can damage ears, eyes, lungs, and skin if precautions are not taken. Wear safety goggles and a dust filter mask when mixing plaster of Paris. Some experts suggest mixing the plaster of Paris when students are not in the room. Use rubber gloves whenever it is practical. Also, plaster of Paris gives off heat as it solidifies. Although it probably could not burn a student, remind everyone to practice safety first.

Plaster of Paris should not be poured down the sink because it will clog drains. Clean all utensils as soon as possible so that the plaster will not harden on them. Whenever possible, use plastic containers that flex slightly. The plaster of Paris will crack and fall off when the container is bowed.

■ Plaster of Paris Dinosaur or Bird Eggs
[Makes 4 eggs]

These "eggs" can be added to dioramas. Sudents can research a certain species' egg size.

Materials

1 cup plaster of Paris	4 small, oval balloons
1/2 cup water	string
disposable mixing bowl	large bucket, half-filled with water
plastic mixing spoon	sandpaper
funnel	paints and paintbrushes

Procedure

1. Mix the water and plaster of Paris together in the mixing bowl. The mixture should be smooth and creamy.
2. Place the funnel in the opening of one of the balloons.
3. Spoon part of the mixed plaster through the funnel into the balloon. The balloon will expand as more plaster is added. The plaster will take the shape of the balloon, but do not stretch the balloon to its limit.
4. Pinch the balloon opening as you remove the funnel.
5. Tie the opening closed with the string.
6. Float the balloon in the water bucket so that there is no flat side.
7. Repeat the process with the other three balloons.
8. Leave the plaster-filled balloons in the bucket for several hours.
9. Remove and dry.
10. Cut away the balloons.
11. Sand off the points where the balloons were tied.
12. Let the "eggs" age for a day or two, then paint them.

■ Sidewalk Chalk
[Makes 4 sticks of chalk]

This chalk is great for hopscotch and sidewalk pictures. Do not use it on chalkboards.

Materials

2 tablespoons powdered tempera paint
1/2 cup water
1 cup plaster of Paris

mixing container
mixing spoon
small paper cups

Procedure

1. Mix all ingredients in a container.
2. Pour into small paper cups.
3. Let harden overnight.
4. Peel off the paper and use.

■ Plaster of Paris Draped Cloth
[Makes about 2 cups]

The stiffened fabric makes excellent ghosts for Halloween or angels for holidays. It can also cover chicken wire for very large projects. The cloth dries fairly rapidly, because the alum causes the plaster of Paris to harden more quickly.

Materials

newspaper
2 cups plaster of Paris
1 teaspoon alum
1 cup water
fabric, sheets, or netting

mixing bowl
mixing spoon
bottle, inverted vase, or other object serving as a stand
paints and paintbrushes (optional)

Procedure

1. Cover entire work area with newspaper.
2. Combine the plaster of Paris and alum in the mixing bowl.
3. Add enough water to make the plaster a thick consistency.
4. Dip the fabric into the plaster of Paris.
5. Remove the fabric and drape it over the stand. Arrange the fabric to suit taste.
6. Once the fabric stiffens, do not rearrange it.
7. Paint the fabric when dry.

■ Plaster of Paris Dinosaur Footprints
[Makes 4 footprints]

A fossil is a hardened trace of an animal or plant. A dinosaur's footprint is a type of fossil.

Materials

petroleum jelly
plastic replica of a dinosaur
1 cup plaster of Paris
1/2 cup water

disposable mixing bowl
plastic mixing spoon
waxed paper

Procedure

1. Coat the dinosaur replica's feet with petroleum jelly.
2. Pour the plaster of Paris into the disposable mixing bowl.
3. Add enough water to the plaster of Paris to make it creamy. Use the plastic spoon to stir it.
4. Spoon the plaster of Paris onto the waxed paper.
5. Wait until the plaster is fairly stiff.
6. Have the dinosaur replica "step" into and out of the plaster of Paris.
7. Let the plaster of Paris dry overnight. Examine the footprints.

■ Plaster of Paris Plant Imprints
[Makes 3 imprints]

Paleontologists have found many fossilized plant imprints. This formula replicates the process.

Materials

fresh leaves or flowers
1 cup plaster of Paris
1/2 cup water

disposable mixing bowl
plastic mixing spoon
waxed paper

Procedure

1. Pour the plaster of Paris into the disposable mixing bowl.
2. Add enough water to the plaster of Paris to make it creamy. Use the plastic spoon to stir it.
3. Spoon the plaster of Paris onto the waxed paper.
4. Wait until the plaster is fairly stiff.
5. Press the fresh leaf or flower into the plaster. Remove.
6. Let the plaster harden for a few hours. Examine the imprint.

■ Plaster of Paris Fossil
[Makes 4 small fossils]

A fossil of a bone is usually not the real bone. The animal fell into a clay-like substance and died. Then the bone rotted away, leaving an impression. Water, containing dissolved minerals, entered the impression over time. Later, the water seeped out and the minerals remained, filling the impression. Eventually the minerals hardened into the shape of the original bone.

Materials

waxed paper
1 cup soft clay that will not
  harden overnight
item to make a fossil imprint
  (e.g., a clean bone or stick)

petroleum jelly
1 cup plaster of Paris
1/2 cup water
disposable mixing bowl
plastic mixing spoon

Procedure

1. Lay the clay on the waxed paper. Make sure the clay is soft and pliable.
2. Coat the bone, stick, or other object with petroleum jelly.
3. Press the object into the clay, then remove it. Make sure it has left a good imprint.
4. Coat the imprint with petroleum jelly.
5. Pour the plaster of Paris into the disposable mixing bowl.
6. Add enough water to the plaster of Paris to make it creamy. Use the plastic spoon to stir it.
7. Pour the plaster of Paris over the clay and imprint. Let it harden overnight.
8. The next day, peel off the clay. The fossil is now complete.

■ Fresco
[Makes 1 fresco—enough for 1 student]

A fresco is a painting that is painted into the wall. First, the artist draws the work on paper. This paper is called a cartoon. Then a layer of plaster is applied to a wall. The cartoon is laid against the plaster and traced. Next, the artist applies the paints onto the plaster. When the plaster dries, the pigments become part of the plaster and thus part of the wall. Michelangelo and Diego Rivera are among the artists who became masters of the fresco technique.

Materials

1 cup plaster of Paris	plastic-coated paper plate
1/2 cup water	toothpicks
disposable mixing bowl	tempera paints
plastic mixing spoon	

Procedure

1. Mix the water and plaster of Paris together in the mixing bowl. The mixture should be smooth and creamy.
2. Pour the plaster mixture onto the paper plate.
3. Let the mixture harden somewhat.
4. While the mixture hardens, plan a design for the fresco.
5. Using a toothpick, outline the design on the hardening plaster.
6. Using another toothpick, mix some of the tempera paint into the plaster. The plaster and the paint are now one.
7. Using a different toothpick for each new color of paint, complete the fresco.
8. Allow it to harden and remove it from the plate.

■ Mosaics
[Makes 5 mosaics]

A mosaic is an art form dating back to ancient Mesopotamia. Mosaic artifacts have been discovered in many cultures, ranging from Persian Muslims to Mayan Indians. In a mosaic, small pieces of stone or other materials are embedded in mortar. In this project, the plaster of Paris serves as the mortar.

Materials

2 cups plaster of Paris
1 cup water
disposable mixing bowl
plastic mixing spoon

5 aluminum pie plates
   (8-inch diameter)
items to embed in the mosaic
   (e.g., shells, beans, pinecones)

Procedure

1. Mix the water and plaster of Paris together in the mixing bowl. The mixture should be smooth and creamy.
2. Pour the plaster mixture into the aluminum pans.
3. Let the mixture harden somewhat.
4. While the mixture hardens, plan a design for the mosaic.
5. When the mixture is fairly stiff, embed the items according to the plan.
6. Let the mosaic harden for several hours. Remove it from the pan.

■ Faux Marble
[Makes 1 project]

The glue strengthens the plaster of Paris. The tempera-paint coloring allows for creativity.

Materials

1/2 cup water
1 tablespoon white glue
1 cup plaster of Paris
tempera paint

mixing bowl
mixing spoon
plaster of Paris mold, made of plastic or
   rubber (can be purchased at craft stores
   or through art supply catalogs)

Procedure

1. Combine the white glue and water in the mixing bowl.
2. Add enough plaster of Paris to make a mixture the consistency of mashed potatoes.
3. Pour the tempera paint on top of plaster of Paris. With mixing spoon, swirl paint into the plaster of Paris.
4. Pour into the mold and let it harden. Release from the mold.

■ Volcano
[Makes 1 volcano]

Follow the procedure below to make the volcano. See chapter 12 for the procedure for "activating" the volcano.

Materials

jar	mixing container
flat pan	1 cup water
small square of aluminum foil to cover the mouth of the jar	spoon
2 cups plaster of Paris	paints and paintbrushes

Procedure

1. Place the jar in the middle of the pan. Cover the mouth of the jar with the aluminum foil.

2. Pour the plaster of Paris into the mixing container. Add water and stir.

3. When the plaster is fairly stiff, pour it over the jar. Scrape away any plaster that is directly on the aluminum foil.

4. Using the spoon, sculpt the plaster so that it looks like the sides of a volcano. Let harden.

5. Cut the aluminum foil to reveal the inside of the jar. The mouth of the jar is the mouth of the volcano.

6. Paint the volcano.

5
Glues and Pastes

■ Papier-Mâché Paste
[Makes 2 quarts]

Papier-mâché paste obviously is great for papier-mâché projects. Warm it slightly before using it. It also can be thinned with water and used as a more traditional paste.

Materials

2 cups flour
1/4 cup sugar
2 quarts warm water
1/2 teaspoon oil of cinnamon
  (to act as preservative)*

stove, heating element, or
  microwave
pot or microwave-safe container
mixing spoon
storage container with lid

*Oil of cinnamon should not be eaten. If small students use this material, consider leaving the oil out. It is available at health food stores.

Procedure

1. Combine the flour and sugar.
2. Add a bit of warm water to make a thick paste. Slowly add the rest of the water, stirring with each addition.
3. Boil, stirring continuously, until the mixture is thick and clear. Or, microwave the mixture at high setting for 2 minutes, stir, and microwave again at high setting for 2 minutes.
4. Add the oil of cinnamon.
5. Pour into the storage container.

■ Decoupage and Collage Glue
[Makes 2 cups]

Decoupage takes several days. Each application of glue must thoroughly dry before another layer is added.

Materials

1-1/2 cups white glue
1/2 cup water

container
mixing spoon

Procedure

1. Combine the glue and water in the container.
2. Apply one layer of glue for collage. Add several more layers for decoupage.

■ Emergency Paste
[Makes 2 cups]

Make this paste when students want glue "now" and all the white glue has disappeared.

Materials

1/2 cup flour
3/4 cup cold water
1 cup boiling water
mixing bowl

mixing spoon
stove or heating element
pot
airtight container with lid

Procedure

1. Combine the flour and cold water in the mixing bowl.
2. Pour the mixture into the boiling water.
3. Cook, stirring continuously, for 3 minutes.
4. Cool and store in the container.

■ Paper Paste
[Makes 2 cups]

Papers glued with this paste will dry flat. Sometimes commercial white glues "buckle" paper.

Materials

9 ounces white dextrin
   (available at grocery stores in
   the artificial sweeteners section)
1-3/4 cups water
2 teaspoons sugar
2 teaspoons glycerin

1 teaspoon alum
candy thermometer
stove or heating element
pot
mixing spoon
airtight container with lid

Procedure

1. Combine the dextrin and water in the pot. Heat to 140°, stirring constantly.
2. Add the other ingredients and heat until the mixture becomes clear.
3. Let the mixture cool slightly and then pour it into an airtight container. Let cool completely.

■ Non-Paper Glue
[Makes 1/2 cup]

Use this glue in its liquid state to attach glass to glass or wood to wood. It will bond metal to metal when it is gelled.

Materials

2 envelopes unflavored gelatin	small mixing bowl
1-1/2 tablespoons water	mixing spoon
3 tablespoons skim milk	stove or heating element
1/4 teaspoon oil of cinnamon	pot
(to act as preservative)*	storage container

*Oil of cinnamon should not be eaten. If small students use this material, consider leaving the oil out. It is available at health food stores.

Procedure

1. In the small mixing bowl, combine the gelatin and water.
2. In the pot, scald the skim milk.
3. Pour the milk into the gelatin mixture.
4. Add the oil of cinnamon if desired.
5. Pour into the storage container.
6. The glue will gel in the container. To liquefy, place the container into a larger receptacle containing a bit of hot water.

■ Colored Glues

Glue makers are now selling colored glues. The colored glues add spice to posters and other projects. Colored glues are easy to make. The following formula is especially great if only a small amount of one color is needed.

Materials

white glue in squeeze bottles	poster paints

Procedure

1. Open the bottles of glue.
2. Add a bit of poster paint to each bottle. Replace the lid and shake. The finished product will be darker colored than the original paint. Do not add too much paint.
3. For a variation, do not shake the bottle too much. The marbled glue will produce interesting results.

6
Paints

Paint is made by combining a pigment (color) with a binder (viscous material). The binder makes the pigment adhere to the support (paper, wood, or other materials). Four types of pigment are nontoxic and are thus safe for students to use. Food coloring is transparent; however, it will not always wash out of clothing. Watercolors are transparent and usually washable. Tempera and poster paints are more opaque. They are reasonably priced and easy to obtain, and they often wash out of clothing. Acrylics are opaque but expensive, and they often do not wash out of clothing. In many of the following formulas, pigments can be changed to meet the need for transparency or opacity.

■ Transparent Finger Paint
[Makes 3-1/4 cups]

This shiny, transparent paint can be used on either wet or dry paper. It dries more quickly than other finger paints. Leftover paint lasts about one week if refrigerated. It can be used for painting windows. However, it is not as easy to remove from glass surfaces as are other paints.

Materials

1 tablespoon (1 envelope) unflavored gelatin	mixing bowl
3 cups water	mixing spoon
1/2 cup cornstarch	stove, heating element, or microwave
4 tablespoons dishwashing liquid	pot or microwave-safe container
food coloring	small containers with lids

Procedure

1. In a mixing bowl, add the gelatin to 1/2 cup of water.
2. Pour the cornstarch into the pot and add 2-1/2 cups cold water. The cornstarch should dissolve. Simmer and stir until thick. Take the pot off the heat. Or, microwave the mixture at medium setting for 2 minutes, stir, and microwave again at medium setting for 2 minutes.
3. Add the gelatin and then the dishwashing liquid to the mixture in the pot. Let it cool.
4. Pour into small jars. Add food coloring to obtain desired shades.
5. Cover and store at room temperature.

■ Somewhat-Opaque Finger Paint
[Makes 2-1/2 cups]

This finger paint flows smoothly, and it can be used on either wet or dry paper. It is much more opaque than the transparent finger paint described above. The flour produces a smell that may bother some students. A bit of vanilla flavoring or lemon extract will mask the smell.

Materials

1/2 cup flour	poster paints or dry tempera paints
2 cups water	stove, heating element, or microwave
1 tablespoon glycerin	pot or microwave-safe container
vanilla flavoring or lemon extract	mixing spoon
1 teaspoon borax*	small containers with lids

*Borax may be toxic if swallowed. If this project is for small students, do not use borax. Borax is a preservative. Therefore, paints without borax must be used fairly quickly.

Procedure

1. In the pot, combine the flour with enough water to make a paste.
2. Add the rest of the water, and stir over low heat until the mixture is thick. Let cool. Or, microwave the mixture at high setting for 1-1/2 minutes, stir, and microwave again at high setting for 1-1/2 minutes.
3. Add glycerin, flavoring, and borax.
4. Pour into small jars and let cool. Add the poster paints or tempera paints to obtain desired shades.

■ Opaque Finger Paint
[Makes 1 cup]

This paint is fun to feel and easy to use. It will layer over other colors.

Materials

1 cup liquid starch	mixing bowl
2 tablespoons cornstarch	mixing spoon
acrylic paints	small containers with lids

Procedure

1. Combine the liquid starch and cornstarch in the mixing bowl.
2. Pour into small containers and add acrylic paints until the desired color is reached.
3. Cover tightly when not in use.

■ Versatile Paint

[Makes 4 small containers of paint]

Versatile paint makes a great finger paint as well as a poster-type paint. It has only two ingredients and will keep for a long time. It gives a transparent, flat finish.

Materials

2 cups liquid starch
1 cup each of 4 shades of
  dry tempera paint

mixing spoon
4 small, airtight containers with lids

Procedure

1. Pour the liquid starch into the small containers.

2. Add the dry paints, a different color to each container.

3. Blend the ingredients in each container until mixed.

■ Milk Paint

[Makes 1-1/2 cups]

The early American colonists used milk paint to give wood a stained look. Milk was cheap and easy to obtain then. This version produces pastel but vibrant shades. The finish is flat and transparent. Layering it over other colors is fun.

Materials

3/4 cup powdered nonfat milk
1/2 cup water
powdered tempera paints
mixing bowl

mixing spoon
small containers with lids
refrigerator

Procedure

1. Dissolve the powdered milk in the water.

2. Pour into the small containers and add powdered paints until the desired color is reached.

3. Store in the refrigerator. This paint does not last long, however, even in a refrigerator. Use it as soon as possible.

■ Glue Paint
[Makes 1-3/4 cups]

Use this opaque paint to cover waxy or plastic surfaces. It has a flat finish.

Materials

1 cup white glue
acrylic paints
1/2 cup water

mixing spoon
small containers with lids

Procedure

1. Pour the glue into the small containers and add acrylic paints to obtain desired colors.

2. Mix glue and paints. Test to see if the desired color is achieved.

3. Make sure the lids are on tight when the paints are not in use.

■ Egg Tempera Paint
[Makes 1-1/4 cups]

Egg tempera is a medium that has been used by painters from Michelangelo to Andrew Wyeth. It is opaque but can be thinned to any level of transparency by adding water. Although it is thick enough to be a good paint for windows, it is not easy to remove.

Materials

1/2 cup egg yolks (4 egg yolks)
powdered tempera paints
1/2 cup water

mixing spoon
small containers with lids
refrigerator

Procedure

1. Pour the egg yolks into the small containers. Add powdered tempera paints to desired shades.

2. Thin with water to desired consistency.

3. Store in the refrigerator. Use quickly, because these paints will not last long.

■ Pan Paints
[Makes about 2 tablespoons]

The end product is a dry, foamy, transparent paint that can be used like watercolors.

Materials

1 tablespoon vinegar	powdered tempera paints
3 tablespoons baking soda	mixing bowl
1/2 teaspoon glycerin	mixing spoon
(available at drug stores)	small aluminum pie pans

Procedure

1. Combine the vinegar and baking soda in the mixing bowl.
2. After the foaming stops, add the glycerin.
3. Pour into small aluminum pie pans. Add powdered tempera paints to obtain desired colors. The dry paint will be lighter colored than the wet paint. Add a bit more pigment than the final shade desired.
4. Let harden and use.

■ Thick Paint
[Makes 1-1/3 cups]

This paint covers almost anything. For example, it will cover lettering on cardboard boxes.

Materials

1 cup papier-mâché paste	1 tablespoon powdered soap
(see chapter 5)	mixing bowl
3 tablespoons powdered tempera paint	mixing spoon
water	airtight container with lid

Procedure

1. Combine the papier-mâché paste and dry tempera paint.
2. Add enough water to make a thick mixture.
3. Add the soap.
4. Pour into the airtight container.

Black and White Opaque Window Paint ■ 39

■ Opaque Window Paint

[Makes about 1-1/2 cups]

This paint is easy to make and easy to clean off the window when the time comes. It also dries completely. Conversely, the transparent window paint remains rather gooey.

Materials

1 cup liquid dishwashing soap
1 cup cornstarch
food coloring

mixing bowl
mixing spoon
airtight containers with lids

Procedure

1. Combine the dishwashing liquid and cornstarch in the mixing bowl.

2. Spoon into airtight containers.

3. Add food coloring. When judging shade, remember that, when dry, the paint is lighter in color than it appears in the container.

■ Black and White Opaque Window Paint

The colors black and white are hard to achieve with the above formula for opaque window paint. Because those colors are often used, the following recipes solve the problem. If students are painting windows to look like stained glass, the opaque black becomes a great "lead" to separate other colors.

Materials

zinc oxide ointment (available
    at pharmacies)
black tempera pigment (for black)

mixing spoon
airtight container with lid

Procedure

1. Use plain zinc oxide ointment for white paint.

2. Add black tempera pigment to zinc oxide to make black paint.

3. Store paints in airtight containers.

■ Transparent Window Paint

Students love working with the petroleum jelly. This paint does not run, and it can easily be removed if mistakes are made; however, it does not dry to a hard finish.

Materials

petroleum jelly   plastic spoons
food coloring   paper cups

Procedure

1. Spoon a small amount of petroleum jelly into each paper cup.

2. Add drops of food coloring and stir to obtain desired colors. On a window, the paint will appear lighter than it does in the cup, so make the shade a bit darker to compensate.

7
Natural Dyes

People have been dyeing textiles, paper, and other materials with natural stains for over 5,000 years. Three steps are involved in the natural dye process. First, the dye bath must be prepared. During this step, berries, leaves, stems, or roots are simmered or boiled in water. The color-bearing material is often crushed and then strained from the water, leaving the dye bath.

Second, the textile, paper, or other material to be dyed must be prepared. Most materials, such as clays, papier-mâché, or handmade paper, need little preparation. However, the fibers in fabrics must be treated to keep the dye from fading, washing out, or flaking off. Fibers are simmered in a chemical solution called a mordant. The mordant affects the final dye color as well. Some mordants are poisonous, and all mordants must be handled with care. Students should not handle mordants; therefore, none of these recipes uses mordants. Fibers dyed this way may not be colorfast.

In the third step, the material to be dyed is steeped in the dye bath. Sometimes the material is simmered or boiled in the dye bath. Usually, the longer the material is in the dye bath, the darker the shade will be.

All dye baths should be prepared in enamel or stainless steel pots. Wooden spoons should be used to stir concoctions.

■ Onion Skin Dye
[Makes 1 quart]

This dye is yellow to brown in color.

Materials

1/2 gallon loosely packed, dry skins from yellow, red, or Bermuda onions
1 quart water
stove or heating element

large enamel or stainless steel pot
wooden mixing spoon
sieve
container to collect dye bath
material to dye

Procedure

1. Tear the onion skins into small pieces.
2. Boil in 1 quart water for 30 minutes.
3. Press the skins to get out all the color.
4. Strain the mixture and discard the skins.
5. Let the solution cool.
6. Add the material to the dye. Let soak until the desired color has been reached.

■ Cranberry Dye
[Makes 1 quart]

This dye is bright red in color.

Materials

2 cups cranberries
1 quart water
stove or heating element
large enamel or stainless steel pot

wooden mixing spoon
sieve
container to collect dye bath
material to dye

Procedure

1. Combine the cranberries and water in the pot. Simmer for 15 minutes.
2. Crush the berries and simmer for 15 more minutes.
3. Strain the mixture and discard the berries.
4. Add the material to the dye.

■ Grape Juice Dye
[Makes 1 quart]

This dye is purple in color.

Materials

1 quart grape juice
container to collect dye

material to dye

Procedure

1. Pour the juice into the container.
2. Add the material to the dye.

■ Blueberry Dye
[Makes 1 quart]

This dye is bluish purple in color.

Materials

2 cups blueberries	wooden mixing spoon
1 quart water	sieve
stove or heating element	container to collect dye bath
large enamel or stainless steel pot	material to dye

Procedure

1. Combine the blueberries and water in the pot. Simmer for 15 minutes.
2. Crush the berries and simmer for 15 more minutes.
3. Strain the mixture and discard the berries.
4. Add the material to the dye.

■ Purple Cabbage Dye
[Makes 1 quart]

This dye is blue in color.

Materials

2 cups chopped purple cabbage	wooden mixing spoon
1 quart water	sieve
stove or heating element	container to collect dye bath
large enamel or stainless steel pot	material to dye

Procedure

1. Combine the cabbage and water in the pot. Simmer for 15 minutes.
2. Crush the cabbage and simmer for 15 more minutes.
3. Strain the mixture and discard the cabbage.
4. Add the material to the dye.

■ Spinach Dye
[Makes 1 quart]

This dye is green in color.

Materials
2 cups chopped spinach
1 quart water
stove or heating element
large enamel or stainless steel pot
wooden mixing spoon
sieve
container to collect dye bath
material to dye

Procedure
1. Combine the spinach and water in the pot. Simmer for 15 minutes.
2. Crush the spinach and simmer for 15 more minutes.
3. Strain the mixture and discard the spinach.
4. Add material to dye.

■ Beet Dye
[Makes 1-1/2 cups]

This dye is red in color.

Materials
2 15-ounce cans cooked beets
sieve
container to collect dye bath
material to dye

Procedure
1. Open the cans of beets and strain the beets.
2. Use the juices as the dye bath.
3. Add material to dye.

■ Walnut Shell Dye
[Makes 1 quart]

This dye is brown in color.

Materials

2 cups walnut shells
1 quart water
stove or heating element
large enamel or stainless steel pot

wooden mixing spoon
sieve
container to collect dye bath
material to dye

Procedure

1. Combine the walnut shells and water in the pot. Soak overnight. Boil for 1 hour.
2. Strain the mixture and discard the walnut shells.
3. Add material to dye.

■ Marigold Dye
[Makes 1 quart]

This dye is yellow in color.

Materials

2 cups marigold petals
  (collected at height of bloom)
1 quart water
stove or heating element
large enamel or stainless steel pot

wooden mixing spoon
sieve
container to collect dye bath
material to dye

Procedure

1. Combine the marigold petals and water in the pot. Soak overnight. Simmer for 15 minutes.
2. Crush the petals and simmer for another 15 minutes.
3. Strain the mixture and discard the petals.
4. Add material to dye.

■ Mustard Dye
[Makes 1 quart]

This dye is mustard-yellow in color.

Materials

1/2 cup prepared mustard
1 quart water
container for dyeing

wooden mixing spoon
material to dye

Procedure

1. Mix the mustard and water in the container.

2. Add material to dye.

■ Coffee Dye
[Makes 1 quart]

This dye is brown in color.

Materials

1 cup ground coffee
1 quart water
stove or heating element
large enamel or stainless steel pot

wooden mixing spoon
sieve
container to collect dye bath
material to dye

Procedure

1. Combine the coffee and water in the pot. Boil for 15 minutes.

2. Strain the mixture and discard the coffee grounds.

3. Add material to dye.

■ Tea Dye
[Makes 1 quart]

This dye is tan in color.

Materials

5 tea bags	wooden mixing spoon
1 quart water	container to collect dye bath
stove or heating element	material to dye
large enamel or stainless steel pot	

Procedure

1. Combine the tea bags and water in the pot. Boil for 15 minutes.

2. Remove and discard the tea bags.

3. Add material to dye.

8

Bird Food and Bird Feeders

Bird Food

Birds can be both finicky and fickle when it comes to feeding time (e.g., blue jays prefer sunflower seeds, cracked corn, and shelled peanuts). They will also eat doughnuts and crackers. Woodpeckers choose suet and bacon drippings, but they will consume shelled peanuts if that is all there is.

The most popular kinds of bird food are sunflower seeds, cracked corn, suet, and Niger. Birds that prefer sunflower seeds seem to like the gray-striped variety best. Suet, a white, solid animal fat, can be obtained from the butcher. Place a piece of suet in a mesh bag, such as those grapes come in, or in a suet cage and hang it from a branch. Niger, also called thistle, is far more expensive than other kinds of seeds. Therefore, some people prefer to buy seed blends. Birds also like peanut butter and small pieces of fruits and nuts. Popped popcorn and other seeds, such as those from pumpkins, melons, peppers, and so on, attract birds.

Many birds need grit to help grind food in their digestive tracts. One easy way to provide grit is to crush egg shells. Put clean egg shells in a plastic bag and seal. Then use a rolling pin to roll over and over the shells. It will not take long to break them up. You may also use fire ashes, sand, or poultry grit.

Birds also like water, even in winter. A hose dripping water into a bucket is enough to attract many winged friends.

Finally, coarse salt will bring birds. Place the grit and salt a slight distance away from the food so that birds can choose from a smorgasbord.

Once you start to feed birds, stick with the plan. Birds become accustomed to the supply of food. They particularly need food in late winter and early spring.

■ Bird Food 1
[Makes 5-1/4 cups]

Almost every type of bird enjoys this food. The recipe is easy, and students can do all the work.

Materials

1 pound melted suet or shortening
1 cup chunk-style peanut butter
1 cup rolled oats
1 cup yellow cornmeal
1 cup Niger

1 cup sunflower seeds
mixing bowl
mixing spoon
24 paper muffin liners
muffin pans

Procedure

1. Stir all the ingredients together.
2. Pour into paper-lined muffin pans. Let the mixture harden, and then store it.
3. Peel off the paper before serving the mixture to the birds.

■ Bird Food 2
[Makes 8-1/2 cups]

Because this recipe does not have to dry, students can make the bird-food balls and set them outside immediately.

Materials

2 cups bread crumbs
1/2 pound melted suet
3 chopped apples, including
    skin and seeds
1/2 cup flour
1 cup sugar
1/4 cup cornmeal

1/2 cup raisins
1/2 cup chopped nuts
1 cup peanut butter
1 cup wild bird seed
mixing bowl
mixing spoon

Procedure

1. Stir together all ingredients.

2. Shape into balls and put them out for birds.

■ Bird Food 3
[Makes 6 cups]

This recipe uses only ingredients found in the kitchen. It does not include any bird seed.

Materials

1 cup cornmeal
1 cup uncooked oatmeal
1 cup flour
1 cup wheat germ
1 cup raisins
1/2 cup shortening

1 cup powdered nonfat milk
mixing bowl
mixing spoon
baking pan
shortening and flour to coat pan

Procedure

1. Combine all the ingredients in the mixing bowl.

2. Grease the baking pan and flour lightly.

3. Pour in the batter. Bake at 350° for 1 hour.

4. Let cool. Break into walnut-sized pieces.

■ Hummingbird Food
[Makes 4 cups]

To first attract hummingbirds, make the ratio of sugar to water 1 to 3. After the birds become regular customers, change the ratio to 1 to 4. Wash the hummingbird feeder every week.

Materials

1 cup sugar
4 cups water, preferably distilled
red food coloring

stove or heating element
pot
hummingbird feeder

Procedure

1. Combine the sugar and water in a pot and boil for 2 minutes.

2. Add enough red food coloring to make the solution a bright color. The hummingbirds are attracted to the color.

3. Place the solution in a sugar-water feeder.

Bird Feeders

Birds are particular about foods, and they are selective about where they feed as well. All bird feeders should be near protective bushes or trees.

Many birds (e.g., mourning doves and juncos) feed on the ground. Simply clear fallen leaves or snow from a flat area and scatter some cracked corn.

Another easy way to feed birds is to make feeder trays. Place cafeteria trays on bricks or tree stumps. Spread out some cracked corn, bread crumbs, or any of the above bird foods. Occasionally wash the trays.

Suet attracts many insect-eating birds such as woodpeckers. Place suet pieces in mesh bags such as those that contained produce. Garden supply stores also sell suet cages. Hang the bags or cages from tree branches.

The following bird feeders hang from poles or tree branches or are tied to a tree trunk. They use recycled materials and are easy to make.

■ Pinecone Bird Feeder

This recipe is messy but fun. Students can set up an assembly line and work on these pinecone feeders as a cooperative project.

Materials

peanut butter
assorted toppings, such as raisins,
    sunflower seeds, cracked corn,
    or cornmeal

pinecones
table knife
waxed paper
string

Procedure

1. Spread the peanut butter on the pinecones with the knife. Make sure to get the peanut butter down inside the grooves.
2. Pour the toppings onto the waxed paper.
3. Roll the pinecones in the toppings.
4. Tie a string at the stem end of the pinecone and hang it from a tree branch.

■ Birds' Holiday Tree

The tradition of a birds' holiday tree goes back more than 400 years. This project is a good way for students to help the environment and have fun at the same time.

Materials

popped popcorn
cranberries
cold cereals with holes (e.g., Cheerios®)
needle and thread
oranges, cut in half
grapefruit, cut in half
raisins

sunflower seeds
Niger
small pieces of bread, crackers,
    doughnuts, and so on
mixing bowl
mixing spoon
string

Procedure

1. Pick out a good tree within view of the classroom.
2. Make garlands from the string, popcorn, cereals, and cranberries. Hang them on the tree.
3. Scoop out the pulp from the oranges and grapefruit. Mix it with the rest of the ingredients.
4. Spoon a bit of the mixture back into each orange or grapefruit shell. Attach strings to each shell and hang the shells from the tree.
5. Add some peanut butter pinecones from bird food 3.

■ Hanging Bird Feeder 1

This bird feeder is easy to refill. Students can see how much bird food is consumed in a day.

Materials

empty, clean, 1-liter plastic soda bottle	hammer
plastic plate	large nail
heavy string	music record with a diameter
small, sharp knife	larger than that of the bottle
hot glue gun and glue	sunflower seeds to fill bottle

Procedure

1. Take off the reinforcement from the bottom of the soda bottle. Punch holes along the bottom of the bottle with the knife. The holes should be big enough for the seeds to fall through.
2. Hot glue the bottom of the bottle to the plastic plate.
3. Punch a hole in the top of the cap with the hammer and nail. Place a piece of string through the hole. Tie the string inside the cap so that it will not fall through.
4. Fill the bottle with sunflower seeds. Screw on the cap.
5. Push the free end of the string through the hole in the record. The record will work as a baffle to keep squirrels out.
6. Tie the free end of the string around a tree branch.
7. Wash the feeder occasionally.

■ Hanging Bird Feeder 2

By recycling the plastic bottle, students are helping to preserve their environment.

Materials

plastic bottle with a distinct handle,	craft knife
such as a gallon milk container	wire
or a 1/2-gallon ammonia container.	bird food

Procedure

1. Thoroughly wash the plastic container.
2. On the side away from the handle, cut away a large square of the plastic. The bottom edge of the cut will serve as a perch while the birds eat.
3. Using the wire, tie the bottle to a tree trunk. Loop the wire over a low branch before twisting the wire ends together.
4. Fill the bottle with bird food.

■ Hanging Bird Feeder 3

This bird feeder recycles 1/2-gallon milk cartons. Students can refill it easily.

Materials

wax-coated-paper milk container   sharp knife
   (1/2-gallon size)   wire
stapler   bird food

Procedure

1. Wash the milk container.
2. On one side near the bottom, cut out a large square. The birds can perch there while feeding.
3. Open the milk container entirely, along the ridge across the top.
4. Fill the milk container with bird food.
5. Close the top of the milk carton in its original position and staple it.
6. Poke a hole on each side of the ridge on the top of the milk container.
7. Run a piece of wire through the holes.
8. Hang the wire to a tree by looping one end of the wire over a tree limb and tying the two wire ends together.

■ Hanging Bird Feeder 4

A plastic plant hanger serves as the basis for this bird feeder. Birds can perch on the lip of the drainage tray and nibble at the food that falls through the drainage holes. This feeder is easy to make and easy to refill.

Materials

plastic plant hanger with attached   cardboard disk with diameter slightly
   drainage tray   smaller than that of the plant hanger
aluminum foil to cover the   bird food
   cardboard

Procedure

1. Cover the cardboard disk with aluminum foil. This will serve as the cover to the feeder.
2. Place bird food in the plant hanger. Some of the food will fall through the drainage holes of the hanger.
3. Place the cardboard disk on top of the plant hanger.
4. Hang the planter from a pole or tree branch.

CHAPTER

9
Crystals and Crystal Gardens

Many crystals contain substances that should not be eaten. Discuss safety with students, because the crystal solutions may need a week to produce the desired effects. Crystals are easy to produce, and students like to observe the daily changes. However, the crystal solutions should not be disturbed (stirred, shaken, etc.) after they have been mixed.

The two main ingredients for crystal growing are the chemical (salt, alum, etc.) and water. A saturated solution is made by dissolving as much of the chemical, or crystal material, as possible in boiling water. When the solution cools, it becomes supersaturated. Crystals are a by-product of this supersaturation.

■ Salt Crystals
[Makes 2 cups]

Chemical name: sodium chloride; chemical formula: NaCl. Salt crystals are the easiest and cheapest crystals to grow. Crystals start to appear within 24 hours.

Materials

1 cup salt	heat-resistant jar (e.g., canning jar)
1-1/2 cups water	string
stove or heating element	paper clip, nail, or other small weight
pan and hot pads	pencil or stick longer than the
mixing spoon	diameter of the jar

Procedure

1. Heat the water to boiling.
2. Gradually add some of the salt and stir. Keep the solution boiling.
3. Add more salt and stir. Repeat until the salt will no longer dissolve.
4. Take the pan from the stove. Using hot pads, pour the solution carefully into the jar.
5. Cut a piece of string longer than the height of the jar. Tie one end to the pencil or stick. Tie the paper clip or small weight to the other end of the string.
6. Place the pencil over the top of the jar so that the string and weight dangle into the salt solution.
7. Put the jar in a place where it will not be disturbed. Soon crystals will grow on the string.

■ Epsom Salts Crystals
[Makes 2 cups]

Chemical name: magnesium sulfate; chemical formula: $MgSO_4$. Epsom salts crystals are needle-like and can grow quite large. They are also easy to grow.

Materials

1 cup Epsom salts*	heat-resistant jar (e.g., canning jar)
1-1/2 cups water	string
stove or heating element	paper clip, nail, or other small weight
pan and hot pads	pencil or stick that is longer than
mixing spoon	the diameter of the jar

*Epsom salts should not be consumed. They can be purchased at pharmacies or through chemical supply houses.

Procedure

Use the "Salt Crystals" recipe (see p. 57), substituting Epsom salts for salt.

■ Sugar Crystals
[Makes 2 cups]

Chemical name: sucrose; chemical formula: $C_{12}H_{22}O_{11}$. Sugar crystals are not always a sure thing. Sometimes a syrupy mess is the final product. Some people eat the sugar crystals. However, because the solution has been exposed to germs and other contaminants, eating the crystals is not advised.

Materials

3 cups sugar	heat-resistant jar (e.g., canning jar)
1 cup water	string
food coloring (optional)	paper clip, nail, or other small weight
stove or heating element	pencil or stick that is longer than
pan and hot pads	the diameter of the jar
mixing spoon	blanket

Procedure

1. Use the "Salt Crystals" recipe (see p. 57), substituting sugar for salt.
2. Add a bit of food coloring if desired.
3. Slow down the cooling process as much as possible by wrapping the jar in a blanket.

■ Epsom Salts Frost

[Makes 2 cups]

The liquid dishwashing detergent binds the Epsom salts to the glass. It also allows easy cleaning.

Materials

1 cup Epsom salts*
1-1/2 cups water
stove or heating element
pan and hot pads

3 tablespoons liquid dishwashing detergent
mixing spoon
paintbrush
window or other glass surface

*Epsom salts should not be consumed. They can be purchased at pharmacies or through chemical supply houses.

Procedure

1. Heat the water to boiling.
2. Gradually add some of the Epsom salts and stir. Keep the solution boiling.
3. Add more Epsom salts and stir.
4. Repeat until the Epsom salts will no longer dissolve.
5. Using hot pads, take the pan from the stove.
6. Add 3 tablespoons of dishwashing detergent.
7. Let the mixture cool.
8. "Paint" the solution on a window or glass with a paintbrush. When the solution dries, needle-like fan patterns will appear.
9. To clean, run the glass under water or use a soap and water solution.

■ Baking Soda Crystals

[Makes 1 cup]

Chemical name: sodium bicarbonate; chemical formula: $NaHCO_3$. Crystals emerge within hours. They appear to take on fractal patterns on planar surfaces. Students "ooh" and "ahh" over these.

Materials

1/3 cup baking soda
1 cup water
stove or heating element
pan and hot pads
mixing spoon

heat-resistant jar (e.g., canning jar)
string
paper clip, nail, or other small weight
pencil or stick that is longer than
    the diameter of the jar

Procedure

Use the "Salt Crystals" recipe (see p. 57), substituting baking soda for salt.

■ Borax Stalagmites and Stalactites
[Makes 3 cups]

These formations are not always a guarantee. Sometimes the string dries out, ending the process.

Materials

1-1/3 cups borax*
2 cups water
stove or heating element
pan and hot pads
mixing spoon

2 small, heat-resistant jars of the
   same size (e.g., canning jars)
several 12-inch pieces of light-weight
   string
tray big enough to hold both jars, with
   3 inches of space between them

*Borax, found in the laundry products section of the grocery store, should not be eaten. Watch small students closely when they make this formula.

Procedure

1. Heat the water to boiling.
2. Gradually add some of the borax and stir. Keep the solution boiling.
3. Add more borax and stir.
4. Repeat until the borax will no longer dissolve.
5. Using hot pads, take the pan from the stove.
6. Place the jars on the tray 3 inches apart.
7. Divide the solution between the jars.
8. Soak the strings for 2 minutes in one of the jars. Remove.
9. Place one end of each length of string in one jar.
10. Place the other ends of the strings in the other jar. The strings are thus suspended between the jars.
11. The solution will begin to flow along the strings. Some of the solution will drip from the strings and solidify. Stalagmites and stalactites will form. Sometimes the two features will join and form a pillar of crystal material.

■ Washing Soda Crystals
[Makes 1-1/2]

Chemical name: sodium carbonate; chemical formula: Na_2CO_3. Washing soda is located in the laundry products section of the grocery store.

Materials

2/3 cup washing soda
1 cup water
stove or heating element
pan and hot pads
mixing spoon

heat-resistant jar (e.g., canning jar)
string
paper clip, nail, or other small weight
pencil or stick that is longer than
    the diameter of the jar

Procedure

Use the "Salt Crystal" recipe (see p. 57), substituting washing soda for salt.

■ Borax Crystals
[Makes 1-1/2 cups]

Chemical name: sodium tetraborate; chemical formula: $Na_2B_4O_7$. Borax crystals form against the sides of the jar as well as on the string. They are easy to make, and they start to appear within hours.

Materials

2/3 cup borax*
1 cup water
stove or heating element
pan and hot pads
mixing spoon

heat-resistant jar (e.g., canning jar)
string
paper clip, nail, or other small weight
pencil or stick that is longer than
    the diameter of the jar

*Borax, found in the laundry products section of the grocery store, should not be eaten. Watch small students closely when they make this formula.

Procedure

1. Use the "Salt Crystals" recipe (see p. 57), substituting borax for salt.

■ Cream of Tartar Crystals
[Makes 1-1/4 cups]

Chemical name: potassium bitartrate; chemical formula: $KHC_4H_4O_6$. Cream of tartar is one of the ingredients in baking powder. It is also used to make eggs stiff for meringues and angel food cakes. You can buy cream of tartar in the spice section of the grocery store.

Materials

2/3 cup cream of tartar	heat-resistant jar (e.g., canning jar)
1 cup water	string
stove or heating element	paper clip, nail, or other small weight
pan and hot pads	pencil or stick that is longer than
mixing spoon	the diameter of the jar

Procedure

Use the "Salt Crystals" recipe (see p. 57), substituting cream of tartar for salt.

■ Crystal Garden 1
[Makes 1 crystal garden]

This garden goes through stages. First, buds of crystals appear on the coal. Fairly soon the coal is covered with well-developed clusters of crystals. After a few days the dish bottom displays large crystals. After the solution has evaporated, the crystals turn white and powdery. The whole process takes one week.

Materials

several pieces of charcoal, coal, or sponge	1 cup basic "Salt Crystals" solution (see p. 57)
glass pie pan	1/4 cup vinegar
petroleum jelly	food coloring

Procedure

1. Place the pieces of charcoal or coal in the glass pie pan.
2. Coat the edge of the pan with petroleum jelly to keep the crystals in the dish.
3. Mix the vinegar and the salt crystal solution together. Pour over the charcoal.
4. Dot the surface with food coloring.
5. Let stand undisturbed for several days. Crystals will form on the surface of the coals and on the bottom of the dish.

■ Alum Crystals

[Makes 1 cup]

Chemical name: aluminum potassium sulfate; chemical formula: $AlK(SO_4)_2$. Alum can be purchased at grocery stores in the spice section or at herb specialty shops. It is used to pickle cucumbers and other vegetables.

Materials

2 ounces alum
1 cup water
stove or heating element
pan and hot pads
mixing spoon

2 clean, heat-resistant jars
 (e.g. canning jars)
string
pencil or stick that is longer than
 the diameter of the jar

Procedure

1. Heat the water to boiling.
2. Gradually add some of the alum and stir. Keep the solution boiling.
3. Add more alum and stir. Repeat until the alum will no longer dissolve.
4. Take the pan from the stove.
5. Using hot pads, pour the solution carefully into one of the jars.
6. Let the solution sit for 1 day. Several crystals should appear in the solution.
7. Pour the solution left in the jar into the other jar.
8. Remove the best of the alum crystals from the first jar. This will become a "seed crystal."
9. Cut a piece of string longer than the height of the jar. Tie one end to the pencil. Tie the other end to the seed crystal.
10. Place the pencil over the top of the second jar, so that the string and seed crystal dangle in the alum solution.
11. Put the jar in a place where it will not be disturbed. Soon crystals will grow around the seed crystal.

■ Crystal Garden 2
[Makes 1 crystal garden]

Crystal gardens go back many years. Now one of the main ingredients, laundry bluing, is very hard to find. If you find a cache, corner the market for all of us teachers. The recipe will work without bluing, but the results will not be as dramatic. Pieces of sponge work as well as the charcoal and are much cleaner.

Materials

several walnut-size pieces of brick, charcoal, coal, or sponge
1 quart water
petroleum jelly
glass pie pan

6 tablespoons non-iodized salt
6 tablespoons water
6 tablespoons liquid laundry bluing
2 tablespoons ammonia
food coloring

Procedure

1. Soak the pieces of brick, charcoal, coal, or sponge in water for 20 minutes. Drain off the water.
2. Coat the edge of the glass pie plate with petroleum jelly to keep the crystals in the dish.
3. Place the pieces of brick or other material on the bottom of the dish.
4. Mix all the other ingredients except the food coloring. Make sure the salt is dissolved.
5. Pour the solution over the pieces in the pie plate.
6. Dot the surface with food coloring.
7. Do not move the plate. Delicate crystals should start to appear in 20 minutes.

10
Non-Newtonian Fluids and Slimes

Non-Newtonian fluids fascinate students. These fluids have properties of both solids and liquids. They resemble fluids because they take the shape of their container. They resemble solids because they can maintain a definite shape. Non-Newtonian fluids can clog drains, so never use a sink to dispose of such materials.

■ Non-Newtonian Fluid 1
[Makes 1-3/4 cups—enough for 3 students]

The chemical reaction is quite thick and truly gooey. Students love it.

Materials

4 ounces white glue
jar
1-1/2 cups water
plastic spoon

1 teaspoon borax*
disposable container such as those
    used in delicatessens
food coloring

*Borax is toxic. Monitor its use, and make sure students do not eat it. It can be found in the detergent section of grocery stores.

Procedure

1. Pour the glue into a jar.
2. Add 1/2 cup water. Stir.
3. Mix the borax and the rest of the water in the disposable container.
4. Carefully pour the glue mixture into the borax mixture and mix. Add food coloring if desired.
5. Stir. Drain off extra liquid.
6. Knead until it is pliable.
7. Store in a plastic bag. This dries out after a great deal of use.

■ Non-Newtonian Fluid 2
[Makes 2 cups—enough for 4 students]

This product is similar to commercial "slimes."

Materials

1 cup borax*	plastic, airtight container
1 cup polyvinyl alcohol**	spoon

*Borax is toxic. Monitor its use, and make sure students do not eat it. It can be found in the detergent section of grocery stores.

**Polyvinyl alcohol, according to the manufacturer, is not toxic. However, students should not ingest it. Soap and water will remove polyvinyl alcohol from the skin. It can be purchased from chemical supply houses.

Procedure

1. Mix the borax and alcohol for 5 minutes.
2. Store in an airtight container.

■ Non-Newtonian Fluid 3
[Makes 2 cups—enough for 4 students]

Classic in its simplicity, this formula is a hit with students of all ages. In some ways it will act like a solid. At other times it is a liquid. This will dry out if left exposed. It can be rejuvenated by adding a small amount of water.

Materials

1 cup water	spoon
1-1/2 cups cornstarch	plastic, airtight container
bowl	

Procedure

1. Put the water into a bowl.
2. Slowly stir in the cornstarch.
3. Students really like to mix this with their hands.
4. Store in an airtight container.

■ Non-Newtonian Fluid 4
[Makes 3/4 cup—enough for 1 student]

It snaps! It bounces! It rolls! It picks up the print from newsprint! It is fun!

Materials

1/2 cup white school glue
1/4 cup liquid starch
food coloring (optional)

small, disposable container
waxed paper

Procedure

1. Mix the ingredients in the disposable container.
2. Knead on the waxed paper surface until smooth.
3. If it is too sticky, add a bit more starch.
4. If it does not flow, add a bit more glue.
5. This fluid does not last when stored. Use it the day you make it.

■ Non-Newtonian Fluid 5
[Makes 1/2 cup]

This concoction dries out after a while. However, it is fun to squish and squeeze.

Materials

2 teaspoons white toothpaste
4 teaspoons cornstarch
2 teaspoons white glue
1 teaspoon water

small mixing bowl
mixing spoon
waxed paper

Procedure

1. Combine the toothpaste, cornstarch, and glue in the bowl.
2. Add a bit of water and mix. Add a bit more water until the mixture becomes a ball.
3. Place on waxed paper and begin to knead, roll, and enjoy.

11

Bubble Solutions and Bubble Frames

Most bubble solutions should be made days ahead, preferably one week ahead, of the day you plan to use them. Keep bubble solutions at room temperature. Use distilled water whenever possible. The size of the bubbles depends on such factors as humidity and air circulation. Also, the rule seems to be that less is more where bubbles are concerned. The less soap used, the bigger the bubbles. If bubbles are made indoors, watch out for slippery floors by the end of the project.

■ Bubble Solution 1
[Makes 1 cup]

Glycerin extends the life of the bubble.

Materials

2/3 cup water, preferably distilled
1/3 cup liquid dishwashing detergent
1 teaspoon glycerin (available at most drug stores)

green or yellow food coloring (optional)
mixing bowl
mixing spoon
plastic storage container

Procedure

1. Mix the water, detergent, and glycerin together. Add food coloring if desired.

2. Pour into a plastic container. Allow it to age for a few days if possible.

■ Bubble Solution 2
[Makes 1-1/2 cups]

Corn syrup is cheaper and easier to obtain than glycerin. Like glycerin, it helps bubbles last longer.

Materials

4 tablespoons liquid dishwashing detergent
1 tablespoon corn syrup
1 cup water, preferably distilled

mixing bowl
mixing spoon
plastic storage container

Procedure

1. Mix the ingredients together.

2. Pour into a container and let the contents settle before using.

■ Bubble Solution 3

[Makes 1-1/4 cups]

The gelatin gives this solution a lumpy feeling. The bubbles are large and stable.

Materials

1 cup boiling water, preferably distilled
1 envelope unflavored gelatin
3 tablespoons liquid dishwashing detergent

heat-proof bowl
mixing spoon
plastic storage container

Procedure

1. In the bowl, dissolve the gelatin in the boiling water.
2. Add the liquid dishwashing detergent. Let cool and store in a plastic container.

■ Bubble Solution 4

[Makes 1-1/3 cups]

Bubble solution 4 needs hot water to properly dissolve the honey. Honey is sometimes easier to obtain than either glycerin or corn syrup.

Materials

1 cup hot water, preferably distilled
3 tablespoons honey
4 tablespoons liquid dishwashing detergent

mixing bowl
mixing spoon
plastic storage container

Procedure

1. Mix together the honey, detergent, and hot water.
2. Let the mixture age for a few days.

■ Bubble Solution 5

[Makes 1-1/4 cups]

Some shampoos work better than others. Built-in conditioners seem to help. Pert Plus® is a good choice. One advantage of this shampoo formula is that it smells nice.

Materials

1/4 cup shampoo   mixing spoon
1 cup water, preferably distilled   plastic storage container
mixing bowl

Procedure

1. Mix together the water and shampoo.
2. Let the mixture age for a few days.

■ Bubble Solution 6

[Makes 1-1/4 cups]

This bubble solution is a better choice when you need some in a hurry. The bubbles seem to be tougher than those made with most other solutions. However, it will not keep more than a day.

Materials

4 tablespoons liquid hand soap   mixing bowl
  (not antibacterial)   mixing spoon
1 cup hot water, preferably distilled   plastic storage container

Procedure

1. Mix the hand soap with the hot water.
2. Let it cool and use immediately.

■ Tabletop Bubbles

Students' work areas have never been as clean as they will be after this experiment. Consider having students wear safety glasses, because the bubbles break close to their faces.

Materials

tabletops   straws
bubble solution

Procedure

1. Give each student a straw.
2. Pour 1 tablespoon of bubble solution onto the table in front of each student.
3. Instruct students to put one end of the straw into the bubble solution and blow through the other end.
4. With practice, students can make bubbles bigger than dinner plates. They can also make bubbles inside bubbles and bubble trains.
5. If a student is having trouble getting a bubble started, swirl the solution around until a small bubble forms. Then the student can pierce the small bubble with the straw and blow slowly.

■ Bubble Frame 1

The plastic bubble wands found in commercial bubble solutions are just a beginning to this creative process. Bubble frames can be three-dimensional or square-edged or both. No matter what the shape of the frame, the bubbles will come out spherical. Bell wire is best for these frames because it is easy to obtain and easy to cut. The plastic coating protects students' fingers.

Materials

18 inches of bell wire per student   wire cutters
    (available from hardware stores   1 container of bubble solution
    or science supply catalogs)

Procedure

1. Cut the bell wire into 18-inch pieces, one for each student.
2. Direct students to make a simple frame such as those found in commercial bubble bottles. Try out the frames.
3. Make frames of various shapes (square, triangular, three-dimensional, etc.).
4. Record what works and what does not work.
5. Make a very large frame from the wire. Have a contest to see who can make the biggest bubble.

■ Bubble Frame 2

Science becomes fun with this rectangular but flexible frame. Not only can students blow bubbles, they can manipulate the shape of the frame and thus the bubble film. Outdoors, students can make gigantic frames by using dowels, long lengths of heavy string, and large plastic containers (to hold the bubble solution).

Materials

2 pipe cleaners per student
2 12-inch lengths of string
   per student

shallow rectangular pans filled
   with bubble solution

Procedure

1. Tie one end of a length of string to one end of a pipe cleaner.

2. Tie the other end of the string to one end of the second pipe cleaner.

3. Repeat on the other ends of the pipe cleaners with the second string.

4. The resulting bubble frame is a rectangular shape with pipe cleaners at the top and bottom and string on both sides.

5. Place the bubble frame into the rectangular pan of bubble solution. Allow the bubble solution to soak into the string.

6. Remove the frame from the solution and play with it. Twist, contort, and compress the frame. The bubble solution does amazing things.

7. If students get their hands very soapy, they can pass their hands through the bubble film on the frame.

CHAPTER

12

Volcanic Actions and Other Chemical Reactions

■ Volcanic Action 1 (Strombolian Eruption)

Stromboli is an island near Sicily. Its volcano, rising more than 3,000 feet above sea level, has been active for several millennia. It can erupt constantly for periods of up to several years. Stromboli eruptions are seldom violent—lava and gases flow easily and are not pent up.

In this experiment, the action is quick, producing an abundance of bubbles.

Materials

small jar
large pan
dirt, salt map mixture, or
    plaster of Paris

1 tablespoon baking soda
1 cup vinegar
red and green food coloring
    (optional)

Procedure

1. Place the jar in the middle of the pan. Make a "volcano" shape around the jar with the dirt, salt map mixture, or plaster of Paris. Make sure the jar forms the crater of the volcano.

2. Pour the baking soda into the jar.

3. Mix the vinegar with the food colorings.

4. Pour the liquid mixture into the jar. Very quickly, the baking soda and vinegar will produce carbon dioxide, causing the volcano to erupt.

■ Volcanic Action 2 (Hawaiian Eruption)

Hawaiian eruptions, named after the Hawaiian volcanoes, are fairly predictable. The lava often exits from several vents. Hawaiian eruptions are the least violent.

The dishwashing detergent slows the eruption of this volcano, producing a cascading liquid that keeps its shape longer than does the previous formula.

Materials

small jar	1 tablespoon baking soda
large pan	1 cup vinegar
1/2 gallon of dirt, salt map mixture, or plaster of Paris	red and green food coloring (optional)
	1 teaspoon liquid dishwashing detergent

Procedure

1. Place the jar in the middle of the pan.
2. Make a volcano shape around the jar with the dirt, salt map mixture, or plaster of Paris. Make sure the jar forms the crater of the volcano.
3. Pour the baking soda and the dishwashing detergent into the jar.
4. Mix the vinegar with the food colorings.
5. Pour the mixture into the jar.
6. The dishwashing detergent delays the contact between the baking soda and the vinegar. The overall reaction is longer and not so vigorously "volcanic."

■ Volcanic Action 3 (Vulcanian Eruption)

Vulcanian eruptions get their name from Vulcano, an island near Italy. Inside this type of volcano, thick magma builds up inside a central vent. Ultimately, gases increase pressure under the magma and the magma explodes into dust and large pieces of debris.

Effervescent antacid tablets contain, among other items, sodium bicarbonate (baking soda) and citric acid. The addition of extra baking soda just keeps the process going longer. Although the volcanic reaction in this activity is not as fast as the one in volcanic action 1, the results are more explosive.

Materials

small jar
large pan
dirt, salt map mixture, or
    plaster of Paris
2 effervescent antacid tablets
    (e.g., Alka-Seltzer®)

1 teaspoon baking soda
red and green food coloring
    (optional)
1/2 cup water

Procedure

1. Place the jar in the middle of the pan.
2. Make a "volcano" shape around the jar with the dirt, salt map mixture, or plaster of Paris. Make sure the jar forms the crater of the volcano.
3. Place the tablets, baking soda, and food coloring (if desired) in the jar.
4. Add the water. Watch the effects.

■ Volcanic Action 4 (Peléan Eruption)

Mount Pelée on Martinque erupted in 1902, killing more than 35,000 people. Peléan eruptions, named after Mount Pelée, are the most violent types of volcanic eruptions. The thick magma and gases clog a central vent in the volcano. Pressure builds until a terrifying explosion occurs—hot ash and dust cloud the atmosphere. Often, parts of the volcano itself are loosed in the explosion.

The steam from the boiling water enhances the effects of the large, roiling bubbles. This is a favorite with students.

Materials

small jar
large pan
dirt, salt map mixture, or
   plaster of Paris

2 tablespoons baking soda
red and green food coloring
   (optional)
1/2 cup boiling water

Procedure

1. Place the jar into the middle of the pan.

2. Make a volcano around the jar with the dirt, salt map mixture, or plaster of Paris. Make sure the jar forms the crater of the volcano.

3. Pour the baking soda into the jar.

4. Add food coloring if desired.

5. Pour in the boiling water. Stand back and watch.

■ Pennies of a Different Color

This activity makes ordinary pennies turn green overnight. The vinegar acid combines with the pennies' copper to form a new substance, copper acetate.

Materials

paper towel
1/4 cup vinegar

5 pennies
bowl

Procedure

1. Soak the paper towel in the vinegar.
2. Place the paper towel in the bowl.
3. Add the 5 pennies.
4. Fold the paper towel over the pennies so that the pennies are covered on both sides.
5. Wait a day. Uncover the pennies. They should now be green.

■ Pennies and Nails of a Different Color

In this activity, some of the copper from the pennies will appear on the nail. Some of the iron from the nail will deposit on the pennies.

Materials

1/4 cup vinegar
3 teaspoons salt
5 pennies

1 iron nail
small jar

Procedure

1. Combine the vinegar and salt in the jar.
2. Add the pennies and the nail.
3. Check in 2 hours. Some of the copper should be on the nail. Some of the iron should be on the pennies.

■ Return of the Pennies

This activity works because ammonia is a base. It counteracts the effect of the vinegar, an acid. An interesting side effect is how the color of the ammonia changes.

Materials

pennies from "Pennies of a Different
  Color" (see p. 80)
ammonia

small bowl
paper towel

Procedure

1. Place the pennies from the previous experiment into the small bowl.
2. Add enough ammonia to cover the pennies.
3. Let sit for several minutes.
4. Remove the pennies and place them on the paper towel. The pennies will have returned to a copper color. The ammonia will be an interesting shade of blue.

■ Vanishing Color

Bleach makes color disappear. Bleach contains sodium hypochlorite. When the sodium hypochlorite's oxygen mixes with the dyes, a new, colorless substance is formed.

Materials

6 drops any food coloring
1 cup water

small jar
small amount of bleach*

*Bleach should be handled very carefully. It can damage fabrics and harm skin.

Procedure

1. Mix the food coloring and water in the jar.
2. *Carefully* add a drop of bleach.
3. Observe any color changes. Slowly add drops of bleach until the color disappears.

■ Bouncing Egg

Vinegar dissolves the outer shell of a raw egg, leaving only the egg's inner membrane to keep the egg together. The egg can be gently bounced and squeezed. Keep plenty of paper towels on hand in case it breaks.

Materials

1 raw egg
vinegar

container with lid big enough
to hold egg

Procedure

1. Place the egg into the container.
2. Pour enough vinegar into the container to cover the egg.
3. Place the lid on the container and let stand for a day.
4. After 24 hours, remove the lid. Discard the vinegar.
5. Remove the egg. Its hard outer shell has been dissolved by the vinegar. It will be squishy and rubbery.

■ Testing for Starch

This experiment is great as part of a unit on nutrition.

Materials

waxed paper
different kinds of foods, including
    cut potatoes   slices of bread
    cut apples   crackers
    orange segments   slices of cheese

Tincture of iodine*

*Tincture of iodine is poisonous and flammable. Supervise its use carefully. It can be purchased at pharmacies.

Procedure

1. Place the foods onto the waxed paper.
2. Place a drop of the tincture of iodine onto each food.
3. The foods containing starch will turn purple where the iodine touches them.
4. Foods containing starch include bread, crackers, and potatoes.

13
Invisible Inks

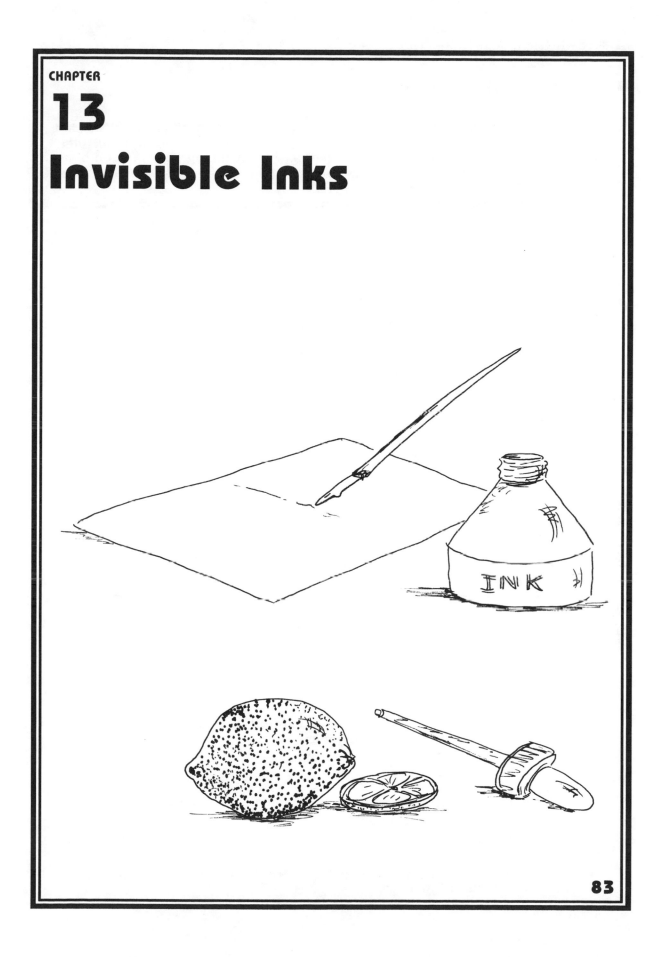

■ Invisible Ink 1
[Makes 1/2 cup]

Students enjoy experimenting with different solutions. The liquid materials are quite safe. Students should be supervised when using the light bulb to prevent burns. A warm iron can also bring forth the messages. However, the iron must be monitored very carefully.

Materials

fine art brush   lamp with bulb
paper
1/2 cup of any of the following liquids:

milk	apple juice
lemon juice	sugar-water solution
grapefruit juice	clear soda
orange juice	(e.g., ginger ale)

Procedure

1. Dip the brush into the liquid.
2. Write a message on the paper. The message should disappear as the liquid dries.
3. To retrieve the message, warm the paper over a light bulb.

■ Invisible Ink 2
[Makes 1-1/2 cups]

Because no heat is required, this process is quite safe. Many students can do the project at the same time. Just watch the ammonia.

Materials

1 teaspoon cooking oil	mixing spoon
5 tablespoons ammonia*	fine art brush
1-1/4 cups water	paper
small container	

*The use of ammonia must be monitored carefully. Do not let students drink it. Watch that it does not splash on anyone.

Procedure

1. Mix the cooking oil and ammonia in the small container.
2. Add the water carefully and stir.
3. Use the brush to write a message on the paper. The message will disappear as the paper dries.
4. To see the message, put the paper into water. The message can appear and disappear quite a few times.

■ Invisible Ink 3

[Makes 1 cup]

With this ink, the message becomes visible when the paper background is stained blue by the tincture of iodine. The message itself does not change color because the vitamin C in the citric acid combines with the iodine to form a colorless compound.

Materials

15 drops tincture of iodine*
3/4 cup water
2 tablespoons citric acid (available at grocery stores; helps fruit retain freshness)

2 small bowls
    (1 should be disposable)
paper
cotton swabs
rubber gloves

*Tincture of iodine is poisonous and flammable. Supervise its use carefully. It can be purchased at pharmacies.

Procedure

1. Combine the tincture of iodine with 1/2 cup of the water in the small, disposable bowl.

2. Combine the citric acid and the remaining 1/4 cup of water in the other bowl.

3. Dip the cotton swab into the citric acid mixture and write a message on the paper.

4. Allow the message to dry.

5. Put on the rubber gloves. Place the message into the bowl of water and tincture of iodine. The message will reappear.

■ Invisible Ink 4
[Makes 1/4 cup]

This method is quite safe and requires no heat. However, it needs a day to let the salt sufficiently dry.

Materials

2 tablespoons salt
1/4 cup water
small bowl

mixing spoon
fine paintbrush
dark-colored construction paper

Procedure

1. Mix the salt with the water in the small bowl.
2. Dip the brush into the salt water solution and write the first letter or two of the message.
3. With the paintbrush, stir the solution and then add another letter to the message.
4. Keep stirring, dipping, and writing until the message is complete.
5. Allow the paper to dry overnight. The message should appear by the next morning.

14
Soaps

People have been making soap for thousands of years. The American colonists made soap by combining rendered animal fat with lye. Making soap from such ingredients can be dangerous. Lye is caustic, and rendering fat requires a fire. Therefore, making soap in traditional ways is not recommended for the classroom. The following recipes and formulas are adaptations of true soap-making methods and will help students understand the process.

Soaps made by the following methods should be used as demonstrations and not as actual cleaning agents. Some skin types may react to these soaps in adverse ways.

■ New Soap from Old Soap
[Makes 4 soap cakes]

In this formula, students recycle soap scraps to see how soap is made.

Materials

1 cup soap pieces cut into small pieces
1 cup water
stove or heating element
steel pan

mixing spoon
oil essences (optional)
small, disposable aluminum loaf or pie pans

Procedure

1. Combine the soap pieces and water in a steel pan.
2. Heat the mixture until it boils.
3. Add the oil essence if you want your soap to have a pleasant smell.
4. Let the mixture simmer, stirring continuously, for 5 minutes. The mixture will take the shape of a ball.
5. Remove from heat and let it cool 10 minutes.
6. Pour into the disposable pans to make the soap into cakes. Squeeze out the air bubbles.
7. Allow the cakes to age for about 1 month. The cakes should easily slide from the molds.

■ Powdered Soap to Hard Soap 1
[Makes 2 cups]

Powder laundry soap becomes hard soap in 15 minutes.

Materials

1-1/2 cups vegetable oil
1 cup powdered laundry soap
   (*not* laundry detergent)
stove or heating element

steel pan with lid
mixing spoon
waxed paper

Procedure

1. Stir the soap and oil together in the steel pan.
2. Simmer for 15 minutes with the lid on the pan. Do not take off the lid until the simmering process is complete.
3. Take the pan off the stove and let cool.
4. When the pan is cool, shape the soap and let it harden on waxed paper for several days.

■ Powdered Soap to Hard Soap 2
[Makes 1 cup]

This formula is easier than the one above. The dissolved soap becomes solid soap very quickly.

Materials

5 tablespoons laundry soap
   (*not* laundry detergent)
2 cups hot water
4 tablespoons salt

2 mixing bowls
mixing spoon
waxed paper

Procedure

1. In one bowl, dissolve the laundry soap in 1 cup of the hot water.
2. In the other bowl, dissolve the salt in 1 cup of hot water.
3. Pour the salt water mixture over the soap mixture. Do not stir.
4. After a while, solid soap will form at the top of the bowl.
5. Remove the solid soap from the bowl and let it dry on waxed paper. This drying may take several days.

■ Soap Balls
[Makes 4 balls]

Making soap balls is fun and simple. For decorative and aromatic purposes only, these balls make good presents for Mother's Day or Father's Day. Students can wrap the finished balls in netting and tie with ribbons.

Materials

2 cups laundry soap, such as
Ivory Snow®
(*not* laundry detergent)
food coloring

scent
2 tablespoons water
mixing bowl
waxed paper

Procedure

1. Pour the soap into a bowl. Add the food coloring, scent, and water slowly.
2. Mix with the hands until a ball is formed.
3. Allow to dry for several days on waxed paper.

■ Liquid Soap to Hard Soap
[Makes 1/2 cup]

The liquid soap will become hard soap very quickly. Students are often amazed to see this process.

Materials

3 tablespoons salt
1 cup hot water
3 tablespoons liquid castile soap
(found in health food stores or
soap specialty shops)

mixing bowl
mixing spoon
cheesecloth

Procedure

1. Combine the salt and hot water in the mixing bowl.
2. Pour in the soap and stir.
3. Within a few minutes, hard soap will float to the top.
4. Remove the hard soap and place in a piece of cheesecloth.
5. Hang the cheesecloth so that the soap will dry. This may take several days.

■ Powdered Soap to Liquid Soap
[Makes 3 cups]

The liquid soap has a slippery consistency.

Materials

2 cups powdered laundry soap
(*not* laundry detergent)
2 cups hot water
2 tablespoons baby oil

scent (optional)
mixing bowl
mixing spoon
liquid soap dispenser

Procedure

1. Pour the laundry soap into the bowl.

2. Add the water and mix. Stir in the oil.

3. Add the scent if desired.

4. Pour into the liquid soap dispenser.

5. Shake once in a while to keep the materials from separating.

15
Candles

Many families in colonial America made candles from tallow. Today, however, most candles are made from beeswax or paraffin. Beeswax candles last longer and give a brighter light than paraffin candles, and they have a lovely fragrance. As might be expected, beeswax also costs more than paraffin. To improve paraffin candles, add some beeswax to the mixture. Just 20 percent beeswax in the mixture makes a difference in the end product. If using paraffin alone, add 3 tablespoons stearic acid (which comes in a powder form) to each pound of paraffin. The stearic acid will reduce smoking and make the candles harder. Both beeswax and paraffin are available from craft shops and candle-making supply houses. Paraffin can also be purchased in grocery stores or from chemical supply houses.

Two different types of wicks, wire and braid, are available in various thicknesses. Use thinner wicks for short or thin candles and thicker wicks for tall or wide candles. Because different manufacturers use differing standards, check with the seller regarding the size of wick necessary for the intended candles. Craft stores sell many materials to facilitate candle making. Items include wick holder tabs, concentrated colors, scents, mold sealers, and mold releases.

It is relatively easy to estimate how much wax will be needed. Decide how much the final candles should weigh. That is the amount of wax to melt.

■ Wax Snow

Because more wax is being applied to an existing candle, wax snow is an excellent beginning candle project. The finished candles brighten a holiday setting.

Materials

beeswax or paraffin	electric frying pan
water	hot pads
3 tablespoons stearic acid per pound of paraffin	eggbeater
	spoon
coffee can	candle with a fairly large diameter

Procedure

1. Put the wax into the coffee can.
2. Pour several inches of water into the pan. Place the coffee can in the electric frying pan so that they act as a double boiler. Slowly melt the wax. Watch out that the wax does not sputter or burn someone.
3. Turn off the heat. Add the stearic acid.
4. Using the hot pads, remove the coffee can of wax.
5. Allow to cool until a film forms on the surface. Beat with the eggbeater until the wax looks like snow.
6. Lift the wax with the spoon onto the large candle. Wax snow can be applied to either the entire candle or just parts of the candle. Do not cover the wick. Let the wax harden.

■ Dipped Candles

Dipped candles are easy to make with large groups. Organize students into groups of three or four. Each student gets one wick, and each group receives one stick. Each student ties their wick to the group's stick. Place the groups in a large circle. As one group dips, the other groups are in different stages of waiting for their candles to harden or waiting to dip again.

Materials

beeswax or paraffin

3 tablespoons stearic acid per pound of paraffin

scent (optional; available in blocks at craft stores)

color (optional; crayons or candle stubs, or purchase in blocks at craft stores)

wicks, 3 inches longer than the desired candles' length

water

large coffee can, deeper than the desired candles' length

electric frying pan

candy thermometer

wooden mixing spoon

wooden stick

bucket, full of room-temperature water (optional)

refrigerator

Procedure

1. Place the wax in the coffee can.

2. Pour several inches of water into the electric frying pan.

3. Put the coffee can into the electric frying pan so that they act as a double boiler. Slowly melt the wax, keeping the wax temperature lower than 180°. Watch out that the wax does not sputter or burn someone.

4. Turn off the heat. Add the stearic acid. Add scent or color if desired. Stir thoroughly, using the wooden mixing spoon.

5. Cut 3 pieces of wick (equal length). Tie each to the wooden stick, letting the wicks hang down.

6. For the first coat, dip the wicks into the wax, let the wicks soak in the wax for 30 seconds, and remove. Let the wax harden. Dip the candles into a bucket of room temperature water between wax dippings, or refrigerate the candles between dippings.

7. Dip the wicks again into the wax. A new layer will be added. Let this layer harden. If the wax is too hot, it will melt the previous layer. If the wax becomes too hard, slightly heat it again.

8. Keep dipping and hanging (15 times) until the desired diameter is reached.

9. Let the candles dry.

10. Cut the bottom of each candle to form a flat surface.

11. Snip the wick knots, and the candles are done.

■ Molded Candles

Craft stores sell two-part candle molds with special releases and wonderful designs. However, lots of items in school and at home make terrific molds. Examples are plastic tubs, milk cartons, and smooth metal containers.

Materials

cooking oil
beeswax or paraffin to fill the mold
3 tablespoons stearic acid per pound
    of paraffin
scent (optional; available
    in craft stores)
color (optional; crayons or candle
    stubs, or purchase in blocks at
    craft stores)
wick, 3 inches longer than the
    height of the mold

mold
craft stick, metal rod, or knitting needle
    longer than the width of the mold
washer (from hardware store)
clay
metal pitcher or coffee can with top
    edge pinched to form a spout
electric frying pan
water
hot pads

Procedure

1. Make a hole large enough to accommodate the wick in the bottom of the mold.
2. Insert the wick through the hole.
3. On the outside of the mold, tie the washer to the end of the wick.
4. Fill the hole with clay so that when hot wax is poured in, the wax will not seep through the hole.
5. Turn the mold over and stand it on its bottom. Tie the top end of the wick on the craft stick, metal rod, or knitting needle. Lay the stick across the width of the mold. Make sure the wick is taut and perpendicular to the bottom of the mold.
6. Wipe the inside of the mold with cooking oil. This will keep the candle from sticking to the mold.
7. Put the wax into the coffee can. Pour several inches of water into the frying pan.
8. Place the coffee can in the electric frying pan so that they act as a double boiler. Slowly melt the wax. Watch out that the wax does not sputter or burn someone.
9. Add the stearic acid. Add the scent or color if desired. Turn off the heat.
10. Using hot pads, pour the wax into the mold, but do not disturb the wick.
11. Let the wax cool for 24 hours.
12. A slight depression may occur where the wick meets the candle. Melt a bit of the wax again and pour around the wick.
13. Let the candle cool again for 24 hours.
14. Put the candle into the refrigerator for a day.
15. Slide the candle out of the mold. If the mold does not give way easily, dip the candle and mold into hot water.
16. Smooth down any rough edges by rubbing the spots with a soft towel.
17. Candles should be allowed to age for at least 1 week.

■ Shaped Candles

These candles are great fun because students can shape the warm wax to suit their fancies. Carefully monitor the temperature of the wax.

Materials

beeswax or paraffin

3 tablespoons stearic acid per pound of paraffin

scent (optional; purchase in blocks at craft stores)

color (optional; crayons or candle stubs, or purchase in blocks at craft stores)

coffee can

electric frying pan

water

wick

carving tools

hot pads

knife

Procedure

1. Put the wax into the coffee can.

2. Pour several inches of water into the frying pan. Place the coffee can in the pan so that they act as a double boiler. Slowly melt the wax. Watch out that the wax does not sputter or burn someone.

3. Turn off the heat. Add the stearic acid. Add the scent and color if desired.

4. Using the hot pads, remove the can of liquid wax from the frying pan and place it on a table or counter.

5. Let the wax cool for 40 minutes, occasionally puncturing the surface of the solidifying wax to allow the liquid wax beneath to cool faster.

6. Test the wax to see if it is cool enough to handle. When cool enough, give each student a portion.

7. Have students manipulate the warm wax by sculpting and carving.

8. Allow students time to figure out what they want to make, then give each student a piece of wick. The candle should be molded around the wick.

9. Let the candles stand for 1 week before using.

10. Trim off the bottom of each candle to make a flat surface.

■ Sand-Cast Candles

A warm, sunny day on a playground of sand is a good place to make sand-cast candles. These candles can also be made indoors, using buckets or small containers of sand.

Materials

sand wet enough to make castles (in small containers or out in the yard)
wick at least 4 inches longer than the desired length of candle
weight such as a washer or nail
craft stick, metal rod, or knitting needle longer than the width of the hole in the sand
beeswax or paraffin
3 tablespoons stearic acid per pound of paraffin

scent (optional; purchase in blocks at craft stores)
color (optional; crayons or candle stubs, or purchase in blocks at craft stores)
metal pitcher or coffee can with top edge pinched to form a spout
water
electric frying pan
hot pads

Procedure

1. Using this method, the bottom of the hole in the sand will be the top of the candle.
2. Tie one end of the wick to the weight.
3. Make a depression in the sand. Poke holes with fingers or kitchen utensils. When satisfied with the shape of the sand mold, bury the weight and the end of the wick. Make sure the wick goes 1–2 inches into the sand. Firmly pack the sand; otherwise, the wax just seeps into the sand rather than remaining in the hole.
4. Tie the other end of the wick to the craft stick or metal rod. Lay the stick across the width of the hole in the sand. Make sure the wick is taut.
5. Put the wax into the pitcher or coffee can. Pour several inches of water into the electric frying pan. Put the coffee can into the electric frying pan so that they act as a double boiler. Slowly melt the wax.
6. Add the stearic acid. Add the scent and color if desired.
7. Using hot pads, pour the wax carefully into the hole. Try not to disturb the wick.
8. Let the wax cool for a day.
9. Slowly take the candle out of the sand. Sand should cling to the candle.
10. Cut the weight off the wick.
11. Turn the candle over. Make sure the bottom is flat.

■ Floating Candles

These candles make a lovely centerpiece for a party table, as well as an interesting science experiment. Pour water into a large heat-resistant bowl (e.g., a punch bowl). Place these small, light-weight candles on the surface of the water (do not float the candles in oil). Light the candles.

Materials

wax snow (from previous formula)   wick holder tabs
muffin tins   (purchase at craft shop)
wick   spoon

Procedure

1. Make the wax snow as described above.
2. Cut the wick into pieces 2 inches longer than the muffin tin cups are deep.
3. Attach the wicks to the wick holder tabs and fasten one to the inside bottom of each muffin cup.
4. Spoon the wax snow into the muffin cups. Keep the wicks vertical.
5. Allow candles to dry and remove from muffin tin.

■ Beeswax Sheet Candles

Students enjoy making these candles. They require no heat, and a whole class can make them at the same time. The candles burn for a long time with little smoking. Sheets of beeswax are about 15 inches long, but they can be cut into shorter lengths.

Materials

sheet of beeswax   wicks

Procedure

1. The beeswax sheet should be pliable. Usually body heat from fingers and hands is enough to soften it. However, it can be slightly warmed in an oven or microwave if necessary.
2. Lay the sheet of beeswax flat on a table. Cut one side of the sheet so that there is a slight slant of 1–2 inches from one side to the other.
3. Place the wick atop the longer side of the sheet.
4. Roll the longer edge of the wax sheet over the wick and keep rolling. A tube of wax forms, with the wick in the center. The sides will slant down from the wick.
5. This candle does not have to age.

■ Egg-Shaped Candles

Egg shells provide molds for these candles. Easy to make, these candles are especially nice for Easter activities.

Materials

raw eggs
wick
scissors
small piece of clay
egg carton
pencil
beeswax or paraffin

3 tablespoons stearic acid per pound of paraffin
water
coffee can
electric frying pan
hot pads

Procedure

1. Carefully tap off the "pointed" end of a raw egg. Empty the albumen and yolk from the shell.

2. Wash out the egg shell.

3. Cut a piece of wick and fasten it to the inside bottom of the shell with a bit of clay. Place the egg upright in the egg carton.

4. Tie the top of the wick to the pencil and lay the pencil across the top of the egg shell.

5. Repeat the process for all the eggs.

6. Put the wax into the coffee can.

7. Pour several inches of water into the electric frying pan. Place the coffee can into the pan so that they act as a double boiler. Slowly melt the wax. Watch out that the wax does not sputter or burn someone.

8. Turn off the heat. Add the stearic acid.

9. Using the hot pads, remove the coffee can of wax.

10. Pour the wax into the empty egg shells. Make sure the wicks remain upright.

11. Let the candles harden. Peel off the shells, or leave the shells in place on the candles as natural containers.

16
Recycled Paper

Paper originated about 2,000 years ago. The Chinese were the first to discover how to make paper. Before that, papyrus, vellum, parchment, bark, and various other materials were used as writing surfaces. By definition, paper is the result of beating plant fibers, bringing forth the cellulose in those fibers, adding water, and sieving the mixture, which is called the slurry.

Making new paper from old paper and other materials is fun, but it is also messy and it takes practice. First products are generally quite thick and resemble the material from which egg cartons are made.

Mold and Deckle

The mold strains the paper fibers from the slurry. It is basically a sieve. The deckle, which snaps onto the mold, frames the new paper and keeps the paper fibers on the mold as it is lifted from the slurry. Mold and deckle sets are available at craft stores and through art supply catalogs. Many book stores currently sell paper-making kits, including the mold and deckle. If you cannot purchase a mold and deckle set, make your own.

■ Traditional Rectangular Mold and Deckle

This process takes the most work of those given here. However, it is probably the most durable.

Materials

window screening, 12 x 14 inches   nails
wood molding   staple gun and staples

Procedure

1. Make two frames from the wood molding and nails. Make one frame 10 inches by 12 inches. Make the other frame slightly smaller.

2. Wrap the window screening around the larger of the two frames.

3. Staple the window screening onto the frame to make the mold.

4. The other frame (without screening) is the deckle.

■ Easy Rectangular Mold and Deckle

Make sure the frames are free of glass and backing.

Materials

2 picture frames (one frame should be slightly larger than the other)	1 piece plastic canvas (7-mesh; available at craft stores)
scissors	hot glue gun and glue

Procedure

1. Cut the plastic canvas to fit on top of the larger of the two frames.
2. Hot glue the plastic canvas onto the frame. This is the mold.
3. The other empty frame will be the deckle.

■ Easy Round Mold

Check craft stores for embroidery hoops.

Materials

pair of embroidery hoops	netting, slightly larger than the larger embroidery hoop

Procedure

1. Separate the embroidery hoops.
2. Lay the netting over the smaller, inner hoop.
3. Place the larger hoop over the netting and snap hoops and the netting together.

■ Very Easy Round Mold and Deckle

The handles on the grease-spatter screens make paper-making tidier.

Materials

2 grease-spatter screens (available in the kitchenware section of department stores)	craft knife

Procedure

1. Keep one spatter screen just as it is. It will be the frame.
2. Cut away the screen from the second spatter screen. It will be the deckle.

Paper and Paper Products

■ Basic Recycled Paper

Plan two days for this project. Students love the mess. They are amazed that they can actually make paper.

Materials

newspaper
warm water
bucket
blender

mold and deckle
dishpan wider than the mold
damp cloth

Procedure

1. Tear the newspaper into pieces the size of quarters. Put the pieces into the bucket.
2. Add warm water to cover the paper. Soak overnight in the bucket.
3. The next day, scoop 1 cup of the paper into the blender. Cover with water. Blend until pulpy. This combination of pulp and water is called slurry.
4. Add more paper and blend again.
5. Pour the slurry into the dishpan.
6. Repeat the process until the dishpan is 1/2 full.
7. Slide the mold and deckle through the slurry until the screen rests on the bottom of the dishpan.
8. With both hands, raise the mold and deckle. A great deal of slurry should stay on the mold as it is raised.
9. Press the slurry to get rid of water and to distribute the material.
10. When the desired shape and thickness are attained, remove the deckle. Flip the mold over the damp cloth. The recycled paper will fall onto the damp cloth.
11. Allow the paper to dry. Remove from cloth.

■ Bleached Paper

Basic recycled paper is rather gray. In this formula, the bleach makes the paper whiter.

Materials

materials from "Basic Recycled Paper" (see p. 103)

small amount of bleach*

*Bleach should be handled very carefully. It can damage fabrics, and it can harm skin.

Procedure

1. Follow the directions for "Basic Recycled Paper." However, add a small amount of bleach to the paper before it soaks overnight.

■ Rag Paper

Rag paper, which contains cotton fibers, is stronger than paper made exclusively from plant fibers. Collect lint from a clothes-dryer filter.

Materials

materials from "Basic Recycled Paper" (see p. 103)

approximately 1 cup clothes-dryer lint for every 1/2-gallon of slurry

Procedure

1. Follow the directions for "Basic Recycled Paper." However, add the clothes-dryer lint to the paper before it soaks overnight.

■ Sized Paper

Calligraphy ink applied to unsized paper will run or bleed. The paper must be prepared to accept the ink. The process of sizing is easy, but the amount of sizing added to the slurry may have to be adjusted.

Materials

1 envelope unflavored gelatin
1 cup hot water
small mixing bowl

mixing spoon
materials from "Basic Recycled Paper" (see p. 103)

Procedure

1. Combine the gelatin and hot water in the small bowl.
2. Follow the directions for "Basic Recycled Paper." However, add the gelatin-water mixture to the slurry before inserting the screen.

■ Multicolored Paper

This recycled paper makes unusual gift wrapping paper.

Materials

materials from "Basic Recycled Paper," except newspaper (see p. 103)

brightly colored paper from catalogs, magazines, and newspaper inserts
several tablespoons white glue

Procedure

1. Follow the directions for "Basic Recycled Paper." However, substitute small pieces of torn paper from catalogs, magazines, and newspaper inserts for the newspaper.
2. Add the white glue to the slurry before inserting the screen.

■ Colored Paper

Because natural dyes are used in this formula, the color may bleed if the recycled paper becomes wet.

Materials

materials from "Basic Recycled Paper" (see p. 103)

natural dye (see chapter 7)

Procedure

1. Follow the directions for "Basic Recycled Paper." However, add the natural dye to the paper before it soaks overnight.

■ Decorative Paper Containers

Recycled paper is somewhat similar to papier-mâché in that it can be shaped over containers. When dry, it takes the shape of the container. This product is not waterproof.

Materials

materials from "Basic Recycled Paper" (see p. 103)
sieve

small bowl, plate, or other container
scissors
paints and paintbrushes (optional)

Procedure

1. Follow the directions for "Basic Recycled Paper." However, do not use the mold and deckle.
2. Remove a cupful of slurry and drain the water using a sieve.
3. Put the slurry in the bowl, plate, or container and press it around either the inside or the outside surface.
4. If the material is molded around the inside of the container, the finished paper container will be rough on the inside and smooth on the outside.
5. If the material is molded around the outside of the container, the finished paper container will be rough on the outside and smooth on the inside.
6. Let stand 1 day. Remove the original container. Trim edges of the paper container with scissors.
7. Paint if desired.

■ Paper from Plants

The plant fibers add great texture and color to the recycled paper. Such paper makes attractive greeting cards.

Materials

several cups of a fibrous plant material, such as onion skins, dried corn husks, celery stalks, day lily stems, iris leaves, pineapple stems

knife or scissors

water

materials from "Basic Recycled Paper" (see p. 103)

pot

mixing spoon

colander

stove or heating element

Procedure

1. Cut the plant fibers into pieces no longer than 2 inches. Place the pieces in the pot.
2. Cover the fibers with water and boil until soft. This process takes about 1 hour.
3. Using the colander, strain out the plant fibers. Rinse with cold water to remove any non-fibrous material.
4. Follow the directions for "Basic Recycled Paper." Add some of the plant material to the blender before adding the soaked paper.

■ Watermarked Paper

Watermarks have nothing to do with water. A watermark is produced by adding a shape to the mold. When the mold is pulled out of the slurry, less fiber is above the shape than the rest of the mold. Therefore, the section on the shape is more translucent than the rest of the paper.

Materials

materials from "Basic Recycled Paper" (see p. 103)

small, flat item such as a washer

small pieces of wire

Procedure

1. Attach the washer to the mold with small pieces of wire.
2. Follow the directions for "Basic Recycled Paper." Look for the watermark when the paper is dry.

■ Embossed Paper

Embossed papers have a raised or textured surface. Embossing may be as simple as an initial or as complicated as a mask.

Materials

materials from "Basic Recycled
Paper" (see p. 103)
second piece of cloth

three-dimensional form, such as
a raised metal letter

Procedure

1. Follow the directions for "Basic Recycled Paper."
2. Couch the paper onto the damp cloth and let it dry for several hours.
3. Place the three-dimensional form onto the second cloth.
4. Place the still-damp paper over the three-dimensional form. Mold the paper over the form to make sure the paper fibers conform to the shape.
5. Let the paper dry thoroughly before removing from the form.

■ Paper from Nature

The natural materials often add an interesting scent to the paper. Students enjoy finding the natural materials in the final product.

Materials

several cups of small, flat, natural
items, such as pine needles,
flower petals, leaves,
herbs, ferns

materials from "Basic Recycled
Paper" (see p. 103)

Procedure

1. Follow the directions for "Basic Recycled Paper." However, add the natural materials to the slurry before inserting the mold and deckle.

17

Dried Flowers, Potpourri, and Pomanders

Dried Flowers

■ Air Drying Flowers, Leaves, and Herbs

Begin the drying process in early fall. Use some of the dried flowers and leaves to make holiday potpourri.

Materials

flowers, leaves, or herbs
rubber bands

Procedure

1. Pick the flowers, leaves, and herbs at their prime.
2. Tie small bunches of them together with rubber bands.
3. Hang the flowers with the petals down in a warm, dark, dry location for several weeks.

■ Drying Flowers with Water

Thick-stemmed flowers such as zinnias dry well with this method.

Materials

flowers   water
vases or bottles

Procedure

1. Pour 1 inch of water into each of the vases or bottles. Stand the flowers in the vases.
2. Allow the flowers to dry. This process may take as long as 2 weeks.

■ Drying Herbs and Small Flowers in the Microwave Oven

Just about any herb or citrus rind can be dried via the microwave oven. Very delicate flowers such as crocus will not dry well this way, however.

Materials

herbs or small but sturdy
  flowers such as daisies

paper towels
microwave oven

Procedure

1. Wash the herbs or small flowers and let them air dry.
2. Place the plants on a paper towel and put them into the microwave oven.
3. Microwave at high setting for a total of 2 minutes. Stop the process and rearrange them on the paper towel every 30 seconds.
4. Check to see if the plants are dry. If not, microwave in periods of 30 seconds until they are dry.
5. Let cool and store in a container with a tight lid.

■ Pressing Flowers

More delicate flowers, such as rose petals, press better than flowers with more bulbous bases, such as zinnias.

Materials

flowers
thin cardboard
heavy books

blotting paper (available at art
  supply stores or by mail-order
  from arts/crafts catalogs)

Procedure

1. Arrange a few flowers between sheets of blotting paper.
2. Cover with a sheet of thin cardboard.
3. Place a heavy weight, such as an old encyclopedia, on top of the cardboard.
4. Leave in a warm, dry location for several weeks.

■ Making a Wreath with Dried Flowers

Students can make small wreaths for holiday gifts. Having several adults present will make this activity easier and safer.

Materials

dried grapevines
large bucket of water
dried flowers
hot glue gun and glue

accents from nature, such as small
   pinecones or cinnamon sticks
wide strips of fabric or lengths
   of wide ribbon

Procedure

1. Soak the grapevines in the water until pliable.

2. Weave the vines together to form the wreath.

3. Tuck in many dried flowers.

4. If desired, hot glue on extra touches, such as pinecones and cinnamon sticks.

5. Tie the fabric or ribbon into a large bow. Attach the bow to the wreath with more ribbon or with hot glue.

Potpourri

Students can be quite creative when they make potpourri. Basically, potpourri is any mix of dried flowers, dried leaves, dried fruit, spices, bark, and herbs. A fixing agent is added so that the fragrances will last longer. Fixing agents include orrisroot, benzoin gum, balsam Tolu, and balsam Peru. Students should choose dried flowers based on their fragrance, appearance, and cost. Rose petals are nice but expensive. Petunia blossoms are cheaper but not as fragrant. Therefore, students might mix petunias and rose petals. Potpourri supplies can be purchased in craft stores.

Potpourri uses fixatives, or fixing agents, to retain fragrance and color. Fixatives should not be consumed. Monitor their use by students.

■ Strawberry Potpourri
[Makes 3 cups]

Students can dry their own strawberries (see p. 161). The red and white colors make this potpourri a charming Valentine's Day project.

Materials

4 ounces dried, chopped strawberries
2 ounces dried strawberry leaves
8 ounces dried petunia blossoms, red and white
1/2 teaspoon cinnamon
2 tablespoons salt
1 ounce powdered benzoin gum
plastic bag
decorative container

Procedure

1. Mix the ingredients together in the plastic bag.
2. Pour into the decorative container.

■ Citrus Potpourri
[Makes 3-1/2 cups]

The orange, yellow, and green colors brighten the potpourri.

Materials

8 ounces dried orange blossoms
2 ounces shredded, dried tangerine peel
1 ounce shredded, dried lemon peel
1 ounce shredded, dried orange peel

1 ounce shredded, dried lime peel
4 ounces dried bee balm blossoms
1 ounce powdered orrisroot
plastic bag
decorative container

Procedure

1. Mix the ingredients together in the plastic bag.
2. Pour into the decorative container.

■ Peppermint Potpourri
[Makes 2-1/2 cups]

This potpourri has a "woodsy" appearance from the brown and gold chrysanthemum petals.

Materials

4 ounces dried peppermint leaves
1 ounce dried sweet woodruff
4 ounces dried chrysanthemum petals

1 ounce powdered balsam Tolu
plastic bag
decorative container

Procedure

1. Mix the ingredients together in the plastic bag.
2. Pour into the decorative container.

■ Spice Potpourri
[Makes 1-1/2 cups]

Spice potpourri's ingredients can all be found at the grocery store. The aroma is lovely!

Materials

1 teaspoon whole cloves
1 teaspoon whole allspice
1 teaspoon star anise
1 cinnamon stick
1 cup rock salt

1/2 vanilla bean, snapped
1 teaspoon vanilla extract
1/2 teaspoon almond extract
plastic bag
decorative container

Procedure

1. Mix the ingredients together in the plastic bag.
2. Pour into the decorative container.

■ Lavender-Rose Potpourri
[Makes 6 cups]

The various colors make this potpourri very attractive.

Materials

1 quart rose petals
2 cups lavender flowers
1/2 cup patchouli leaves
1/4 cup sandalwood chips
1 cup rosemary leaves

2 teaspoons whole cloves
6 tonka beans
1 cup powdered orrisroot
plastic bag
decorative container

Procedure

1. Mix the ingredients together in the plastic bag.
2. Pour into the decorative container.

Pomanders

Pomanders make excellent holiday gifts for parents. They can be hung anywhere to make rooms smell wonderful.

■ Old-Fashioned Pomanders

Colonial children often made pomanders. Because citrus fruits were rare in Colonial times, a pomander was a special gift.

Materials

thimble   oranges, lemons, or limes

For each piece of fruit:
- 100 whole cloves (approx.)
- 1 push pin
- 2 tablespoons ground cinnamon
- 1 teaspoon ground orrisroot
- 2 plastic bags
- 17-inch square of netting (available at fabric stores)
- 1 yard of ribbon (available at fabric stores)

Procedure

1. Poke a hole into the citrus fruit with the push pin. Push a whole clove into the hole in the fruit. Use the thimble to protect your fingers.

2. Repeat this process until the fruit is entirely covered with cloves.

3. Pour the cinnamon into one plastic bag and the orrisroot into the other bag.

4. Shake the fruit in the cinnamon bag and then in the orrisroot bag.

5. Place each piece of fruit on a square of netting.

6. Tie the netting together with ribbon.

7. Hang for 2 weeks to dry.

CHAPTER
18
Breads

117

■ Basic Yeast Bread

[Makes 2 loaves]

Making yeast bread is a great way to culminate U.S. history studies of the Colonial period or the Civil War. Because bread was an important part of the diet during these periods, bread making was an integral household chore.

However, yeast breads are not the easiest breads to make, and they require time and patience. To make whole wheat bread, change the basic recipe by substituting 2 cups of whole wheat flour for white flour. Make rye bread by substituting 3 cups of rye flour for the wheat flour and adding 1/4 cup of caraway seeds.

Materials

1/4 cup warm water (110°)
1 package dry yeast
2 tablespoons sugar
2 cups warm milk (110°)
2 tablespoons butter,
  melted and cooled
1 teaspoon salt
7 cups flour
small mixing bowl

large mixing bowl
wooden spoon
floured surface for kneading
bowl in which to let dough rise
sharp knife
shortening to grease bowl and loaf pans
clean cloth to cover rising bread
loaf pans
oven

Procedure

1. Combine water, yeast, and 1 tablespoon sugar in the small mixing bowl. Let bubble for 15 minutes.
2. Combine the milk, butter, salt, 1 tablespoon sugar, and the yeast mixture in the large mixing bowl.
3. Add 3 cups of flour, stirring after each cup is added.
4. Beat in 1 cup of flour, working the dough until it is smooth and elastic. This takes 5 to 10 minutes.
5. Add another cup of flour, stirring until the dough keeps its shape.
6. Sprinkle 1 cup of flour on the kneading surface.
7. Knead the bread for at least 5 minutes. The longer you knead, even up to 30 minutes, the airier the bread will be.
8. Grease the bowl in which the bread will rise.
9. Put the dough into the bowl, then turn the dough over so that a greased surface is on top.
10. Cover with a cloth. Let rise in a warm area until the volume is doubled (1 hour).
11. Punch the dough down, remove it, and knead it again for a few minutes.
12. Using the sharp knife, divide the dough into 2 parts. Form each half into a loaf.
13. Grease the loaf pans. Place the dough into the pans and again cover and let rise until volume doubles (45 minutes).
14. Bake at 375° until the loaves are crusty and brown (30 to 45 minutes).

■ Corn Bread

[Makes 9 servings]

Indians introduced a kind of corn bread to early settlers.

Materials

1-1/2 cups yellow cornmeal	2 eggs
1 cup flour	mixing bowl
1/3 cup sugar	spoon
1 tablespoon baking powder	shortening to coat pan
1/2 teaspoon salt	baking pan, 9 by 5 by 3 inches
1-1/2 cups milk	oven
3/4 cup butter, melted and cooled	knife

Procedure

1. Combine all the ingredients in the mixing bowl.
2. Grease the pan with shortening. Pour in the batter.
3. Bake at 400° for 35 minutes.
4. Cool and cut into squares.

■ Sourdough Starter

[Makes about 3 cups]

A good sourdough starter should have the consistency of cream and smell wonderful! Sourdough bread was used a great deal by early pioneers and miners in the United States because other leavening agents were very hard to obtain. When settlers were ready to begin baking, they took a portion of the starter to add to the bread dough. They replenished the starter with flour, water, and sugar. This kept the starter active.

Sometimes, the wrong kind of yeast can make a starter thick and smelly. Dispose of it if this happens.

Materials

1 package dry yeast	ceramic or glass bowl
3 cups flour	cheesecloth
2 cups warm water	refrigerator
1 tablespoon sugar	

Procedure

1. Mix the flour, yeast, sugar, and warm water in the ceramic or glass bowl. Cover with cheesecloth.
2. Put it in a warm place for 2 days.
3. Place in the refrigerator until you are ready to use it.

■ Sourdough Bread
[Makes 3 loaves]

Sourdough bread has a sharp, tangy taste. It was a favorite of Yukon prospectors, nicknamed "sourdoughs."

Materials

1-1/2 cups "Sourdough Starter" (room temperature)
3/4 cup milk
2 tablespoons sugar
2 teaspoons salt
2 tablespoons melted butter
5 cups flour
1 package dry yeast
1/2 cup warm water

1 tablespoon butter to grease the bowl
pan
mixing spoon
mixing bowl
bowl in which to let dough rise
floured surface for kneading
cookie sheet
oven

Procedure

1. Scald the milk and then stir in the sugar, salt, and butter.

2. Combine the yeast and warm water in the mixing bowl.

3. Add the starter, the milk mixture, and 3-1/2 cups flour to the mixing bowl.

4. Sprinkle some flour on a counter and knead the dough. Work in more flour until the dough is smooth and shiny.

5. Grease a bowl with butter. Put the dough into the bowl and rub a little butter on the top surface of the dough.

6. Cover and place in a warm spot. Let it double in size (1 hour).

7. Punch it down and knead again. Divide the dough into 3 parts.

8. Cut 1/2-inch slits on the tops of the loaves. Put the loaves on a cookie sheet.

9. Cover with a damp towel. Let rise until double again.

10. Bake at 400° for 10 minutes. Then bake at 375° for 45 minutes to 1 hour.

■ Challah

[Makes 2 loaves]

Challah is often served in Jewish households on Friday nights. It can also be part of "break fasts" for Jewish holidays such as Yom Kippur.

Materials

1 package dry yeast
1/2 cup warm water
7 cups flour
1/2 teaspoon salt
1 cup hot water
1/3 cup vegetable oil
1 tablespoon honey
4 eggs
1 tablespoon water
oil to coat bowl

large mixing bowl
mixing spoon
bowl in which to let dough rise
floured surface for kneading
clean cloth to cover rising bread
parchment paper
cookie sheet
small mixing bowl
pastry brush
oven

Procedure

1. Combine the yeast with 1/2 cup warm water.
2. Mix together 5-1/2 cups flour, the salt, and the yeast mixture.
3. Add 1 cup hot water, oil, honey, and 3 eggs.
4. Knead on the floured surface for 5 minutes. Add extra flour if the dough sticks to the surface. The dough should be stiff and pliable at the end of kneading.
5. Grease a bowl with oil. Turn the dough in the bowl so that oil coats the top surface of the dough.
6. Cover and place in a warm spot. Let it double in size (30 minutes).
7. Place the bread back on the floured surface. Punch it down. Divide the dough into 2 parts. Divide each part into 3 sections.
8. Roll each section into a log, 15 inches long. Braid 3 logs together. Close the ends. Make the other loaf the same way.
9. Line the cookie sheet with parchment paper. Place the 2 loaves on the paper. Cover and let double in volume (30 minutes).
10. Combine the remaining egg and 1 tablespoon water in the small mixing bowl. Brush the loaves with this mixture.
11. Bake at 350° for 45 minutes. The tops should be brown and crusty.

■ Soft Pretzels
[Makes 15 pretzels]

Soft pretzels, the pride of Philadelphians, are often served with mustard. Although students can make traditional pretzel shapes, the coils of dough can become expressions of creativity.

Materials

1 package dry yeast
1 cup lukewarm water (110°)
1/4 cup sugar
1/2 teaspoon salt
2 tablespoons shortening
1 egg at room temperature
1 tablespoon water
3-1/2 cups flour
coarse salt
mustard (optional)

mixing bowl
mixing spoon
2 small bowls
small, covered container
cloth to cover rising dough
grease to coat cookie sheet
cookie sheet
refrigerator
oven

Procedure

1. Pour the lukewarm water into the mixing bowl. Sprinkle on the yeast. Stir to dissolve.
2. Add the sugar, salt, and shortening.
3. Separate the egg, leaving the yolk in one of the small bowls and the white in the other small bowl.
4. Combine half the yolk with the 1 tablespoon water. Cover the container and store until almost the last step.
5. Add the egg white and the other half of the yolk to the yeast mixture.
6. Slowly add 2 cups of flour, stirring constantly. Add more flour until the dough is stiff. Cover and place in the refrigerator until the next day.
7. Divide the dough into 15 pieces. Make coils of dough. Fashion into standard pretzel shapes or original designs.
8. Grease the cookie sheet. Place the pretzels on the cookie sheet.
9. Brush the tops with the egg yolk-water mixture. Sprinkle with the coarse salt.
10. Cover and let rise until double in volume (45 minutes).
11. Bake at 400° for 12 minutes or until nicely brown.

■ Irish Soda Bread
[Makes 2 loaves]

Make Irish soda bread to celebrate St. Patrick's Day. The loaves could be topped with a bit of green icing.

Materials

4-1/2 cups flour
1 teaspoon salt
3 teaspoons baking powder
1 teaspoon baking soda
1/4 cup sugar
1/4 cup butter or margarine
pastry cutter
1 egg

1-3/4 cups buttermilk
2 mixing bowls
mixing spoon
2 pie plates or cake pans
   (8-inch diameter)
floured surface for kneading
oven

Procedure

1. Combine the flour, salt, baking powder, baking soda, and sugar in one bowl. Cut in the butter until crumbly.

2. In another bowl, stir together the egg and buttermilk.

3. Stir the liquid ingredients into the dry ingredients.

4. Knead on a floured surface for 2 to 3 minutes. Make 2 round loaves from the dough.

5. Put each loaf in a greased, 8-inch pie plate or cake pan. Shape dough to fit pan.

6. Cut a cross (1/2-inch deep) on each loaf. Bake at 375° for 35 to 40 minutes or until brown.

■ Basic Quick Bread or Muffin Mix
[Makes 1 loaf of bread or 12 muffins]

This versatile recipe allows for many variations. Make muffins after reading *If You Give a Moose a Muffin* by Laura Joffe Numeroff (HarperCollins, 1991).

Materials

1 egg	1 teaspoon salt
3/4 cup milk	mixing bowl
1/2 cup vegetable oil	mixing spoon
2 cups flour	loaf pan or 12-hole muffin pan
1/3 cup sugar	oven
3 teaspoons baking powder	

Procedure

1. Beat the egg and add the milk and oil.
2. Stir in the remaining ingredients.
3. Bake 1 loaf of bread at 375° for 50 minutes to 1 hour, or 12 muffins at 400° for 20 minutes.

■ Fruit Bread
[Makes 1 loaf]

To the "Basic Quick Bread" recipe (above), add 1/2 to 1 cup fresh, frozen, or dried fruits such as blueberries, apples, raisins, or chopped dried apricots.

■ Orange-Honey Bread
[Makes 1 loaf]

Replace the sugar with honey in the "Basic Quick Bread" recipe (above). Add 2 tablespoons grated orange peel to the batter. Spread orange marmalade on top of the muffins or bread when fresh from the oven.

■ Hearty Grain-Raisin Bread
[Makes 1 loaf]

Substitute 1 cup of quick-cooking oats, granola, wheat germ, or whole wheat flour for 1 cup flour in the "Basic Quick Bread" recipe (above). Add 1 cup raisins, 1/2 teaspoon ground nutmeg, and 1/2 teaspoon cinnamon. Use brown sugar instead of regular sugar.

■ Biscuits
[Makes 9 biscuits]

Serve these biscuits warm with jam. The addition of raisins and a bit of cinnamon gives the biscuits pizzazz.

Materials

2 cups flour
1-1/2 teaspoons baking powde
1/2 teaspoon salt
2 tablespoons shortening
pastry cutter
3/4 cup milk

mixing bowl
mixing spoon
8-inch square baking pan
shortening to coat baking pan
oven
knife

Procedure

1. Combine the dry ingredients in the mixing bowl.
2. Cut in the shortening.
3. Add the milk.
4. Grease the baking pan with extra shortening. Pour the dough into the pan. Evenly distribute the dough.
5. Bake at 375° for 20 minutes. Cool and slice into squares with a knife.

■ Shortcake
[Makes 9 shortcakes]

To the "Biscuits" recipe (above), add 2 tablespoons sugar to the dry ingredients. After placing the dough in the pan, sprinkle the surface with 1 tablespoon sugar. Bake as per the "Biscuits" recipe.

After baking, allow the shortcake to cool. Cut into squares and place on plates. Top with peaches, strawberries, blueberries, or other fruit.

■ Scones
[Makes 16 scones]

Scones are closely related to biscuits. Most scones are a bit sweeter than biscuits. Also, scone recipes usually include eggs while biscuit recipes most often do not. Make and serve scones after reading something very British (e.g., *The Lion, the Witch and the Wardrobe* by C. S. Lewis).

Materials

2 cups flour
2 teaspoons baking powder
1/2 teaspoon baking soda
8 tablespoons (1 stick) butter,
   cut into small pieces
2 tablespoons sugar
1 egg
3/4 cup buttermilk
floured surface for kneading

2 tablespoons sugar to sprinkle
   on dough surface
mixing bowl
mixing spoon
pastry cutter
knife
baking sheet
oven

Procedure

1. Combine the dry ingredients in the mixing bowl.
2. Cut in the butter.
3. Add the buttermilk. Stir until the dough forms a ball.
4. Remove the dough from the bowl and place on the floured surface. Knead for 1 minute.
5. Divide the dough into 2 parts. Form each half into a circle with a diameter of 6 inches.
6. With the knife cut each circle into 8 parts. Sprinkle each wedge with a bit of sugar.
7. Carefully transfer each piece onto the baking sheet.
8. Bake at 375° for 18 to 20 minutes.

■ Hardtack

[Makes 15 large hardtacks]

Sixteenth-century sailors lived on a diet of primarily salt beef and hardtack (dry biscuits). Hardtack was also an important food for soldiers during the Civil War. Diaries indicate hardtack was eaten even when infested with insects. This recipe comes from a Civil War buff.

Materials

4 cups flour
2 teaspoons salt
1/2 cup shortening
1 cup water
pastry cutter
mixing bowl
mixing spoon
floured surface for kneading

rolling pin
knife
spatula
baking sheets
oven
very clean handle from a watercolor
   paintbrush

Procedure

1. Combine the flour and salt together in the mixing bowl.
2. Cut in the shortening.
3. Mix in the water.
4. Turn the dough onto the floured surface and knead until the dough resembles clay. Roll into a 1/2-inch thick sheet.
5. Cut into 3-by-3-inch squares.
6. With the spatula transfer the hardtack to the baking sheets.
7. With the paintbrush handle, make 4 rows of 4 holes each in each square. Make sure the holes go completely through the hardtack.
8. Bake at 400° for 40 minutes or until golden brown.
9. Cool and serve. Store any remaining hardtack in an airtight container.

■ Corn Tortillas
[Makes 15 tortillas]

Tortillas can be eaten alone. However, they are usually the base for such dishes as tacos, burritos, and enchiladas.

Materials

2-1/2 cups corn flour (also known as masa harina, available in grocery stores and gourmet stores)
1/2 teaspoon salt
1-1/2 cups lukewarm water
mixing bowl
mixing spoon
floured surface for kneading
waxed paper
rolling pin
electric frying pan
spatula

Procedure

1. Combine the corn flour and salt. Pour in 1 cup water and stir.

2. Remove the dough and knead it on the floured surface. Add more flour if needed until the dough is not sticky.

3. Divide the dough into 15 pieces.

4. Place a piece between sheets of waxed paper. With the rolling pin, form the dough into a flat, circular shape 4 inches in diameter. Repeat the process until all the tortillas are made.

5. Place a tortilla in the frying pan and cook at a hot temperature for 2 minutes. Then flip and brown the other side. Repeat the process until all the tortillas are cooked.

■ Journey Cakes (also called Johnny Cakes)
[Makes 15 dollar-size cakes]

Both Indians and pioneers ate journey cakes. Nutritious and easy to make, the bread traveled well. Original recipes used dried corn. This adaptation uses cornmeal. The final product resembles a pancake and can be served with jam or honey.

Materials

1-1/4 cups milk	electric frying pan
2 eggs	vegetable oil spray to coat
1 cup cornmeal	electric frying pan
1 teaspoon sugar	spatula
mixing bowl	jam or honey (optional)
mixing spoon	

Procedure

1. Combine the milk and eggs in the mixing bowl.
2. Add the dry ingredients.
3. Coat the cooking surface of the frying pan with vegetable oil spray and heat it to 350°.
4. Pour 4 small amounts of batter into the frying pan.
5. Let the first side brown. Using a spatula, flip the cakes onto the other side.
6. Let the other side brown. Remove from pan.
7. Repeat steps 4 through 6 until all the batter is cooked.
8. Serve with jam or honey, if desired.

19
Edible Art

■ Peanut Butter Clay
[Makes 4 cups—enough for 4 students]

Students can make great animals from this concoction. They can add hair (shredded coconut), eyes (raisins), and many other edible details.

Materials

2 cups peanut butter
1 cup honey
3 cups instant dry milk
bowl
spoon

waxed paper
extra edibles, such as raisins,
    shredded coconut, chocolate
    chips (optional)
refrigerator

Procedure

1. Mix the peanut butter and honey.

2. Add the dry milk a bit at a time.

3. Thoroughly mix and refrigerate overnight.

4. Mold on a waxed paper surface, decorate, and then eat the creation!

■ Granola Clay
[Makes 3 cups—enough for 3 students]

The granola imparts a hearty, substantial feeling to this edible clay.

Materials

1/2 cup maple-flavored syrup
1 cup peanut butter
2 cups instant dry milk
1 cup granola

mixing bowl
mixing spoon
waxed paper

Procedure

1. Combine the syrup and peanut butter in the mixing bowl.

2. Add the instant milk and granola.

3. Give each student a small amount of the mixture. The students can then knead the mixture until smooth.

4. This makes great snowmen. Let the students eat their creations.

■ Marzipan
[Makes 1-1/2 cups—enough for 2 students]

Marzipan dates back to at least medieval times, when a feast often concluded with large marzipan sculptures.

Materials
1 can (8 ounces) almond paste (found in baking section of grocery store)

1 cup confectioners' sugar

2 tablespoons light corn syrup

bowl

spoon

waxed paper

Procedure
1. Break the almond paste into smaller pieces and place in the bowl.
2. Gradually stir in the confectioners' sugar and light corn syrup.
3. Knead on waxed paper until smooth.
4. Break into pieces so that each student can mold and sculpt.
5. Let the shapes dry.
6. Students can eat their sculptures!

■ Frosting Clay
[Makes 2 cups—enough for 6 students]

Students love to "dig into" this clay. It has a wonderful consistency.

Materials
1 container prepared frosting

1 cup confectioners' sugar

mixing bowl

mixing spoon

waxed paper

Procedure
1. Empty the frosting into the mixing bowl.
2. Add confectioners' sugar and mix until a stiff dough appears.
3. Give each student a dab of the material. Let them mold it and then eat.

■ Cheese Clay
[Makes 2-1/2 cups—enough for 5 students]

Because of the color of the cheese, this clay makes great Halloween monsters and such.

Materials

10 crackers
1 small container of processed
    cheese spread
1/2-gallon plastic bag

rolling pin
mixing bowl
mixing spoon
waxed paper

Procedure

1. Place the crackers in the plastic bag and close.
2. Using the rolling pin, crush the crackers into crumbs.
3. Empty the cheese into the mixing bowl.
4. Add enough cracker crumbs to form a good clay.
5. Give each student a dab of the material. Let them mold the clay on waxed paper and then eat.

■ Edible Finger Paints

Young children can practice writing their letters in a very fun, edible way!

Materials

large graham cracker squares
spoons
any of the following "paints":
    prepared instant puddings
    dissolved, flavored gelatin
    whipped cream
    fruit-flavored yogurt
    chocolate syrup

waxed paper

Procedure

1. Cover the work area with waxed paper.
2. On the waxed paper, place a large graham cracker square for each student.
3. Dab a spoonful of one of the "paints" onto the graham cracker.
4. Have students finger paint on their crackers.
5. Then let them eat their creations.

■ Mashed Potato Mountains

This goo enlivens a lesson on geography and land features!

Materials

real or instant mashed potatoes   forks and spoons
   (warm)   plates
warm gravy

Procedure

1. Give each student a plate, a fork, a spoon, and a portion of mashed potatoes. Have each student create "land features," including mountains, valleys, and mesas. Students may use their hands to sculpt the land features.

2. Have each student predict what will happen when gravy, representing rainfall, is poured on.

3. Pour the gravy on the potatoes and record the results.

4. Eat the results.

■ Gelatin Creations

Here the gelatin represents the earth. The dinosaurs are the fossils. The students are the paleontologists.

Materials

8-ounce package of flavored gelatin,   mixing spoon
   preferably a dark red color   clear plastic cups
2 cups water   plastic spoons
dinosaur-shaped fruit snacks   stove or microwave oven
   (available in grocery stores)   refrigerator
mixing bowl

Procedure

1. Make the flavored gelatin according to directions.
2. Let it partially set in the mixing bowl.
3. Spoon partially set gelatin into the clear plastic cups.
4. Stir in the dinosaur-shaped fruit snacks.
5. Place the cups in the refrigerator and let the gelatin completely set.
6. At serving time, the students can become paleontologists. After they discover the "fossils," they can eat them.

Gingerbread Houses

Students enjoy making gingerbread houses. Make "Gingerbread House Templates" first (below). Prepare "Gingerbread Dough" (see p. 136) and "Royal Icing" (below). Directions for constructing the houses are on page 137. Plan lots of time for this activity.

■ Gingerbread House Templates

These templates make a very simple, basic house. As students become more expert, they can make churches, stores, or whatever strikes their imagination.

Make waxed-paper templates as follows:

1. Cut 2 pieces of waxed paper, 7-1/2 by 4-1/4 inches. One piece will be the front, and one piece will be the back. Cut windows and doors in the waxed paper as desired.

2. Cut 2 pieces of waxed paper for sides of the house: each piece should have 5 edges and be shaped for a house with a peak. The rectangular bottom of each piece should be 7 by 4-1/4 inches. The triangular peak portion should be 7 inches wide and 4-1/4 inches high. Cut windows in the waxed paper as desired.

3. Cut 2 pieces of waxed paper, 9 by 6-1/4 inches, to serve as roof sections.

■ Royal Icing
[Makes enough for 1 house]

Royal icing is not tasty. Because royal icing dries very hard, it serves as mortar, joining gingerbread pieces together.

Materials

3 egg whites (save yolks for egg tempera paints; see chapter 6)
1/2 teaspoon cream of tartar
1 pound confectioners' sugar

mixing bowl with electric mixer
mixing spoon
refrigerator

Procedure

1. Combine ingredients in the mixing bowl.

2. Beat at high speed until somewhat stiff peaks form.

3. Start gluing!

4. Unused icing can be refrigerated for 2 days in a container with a tight lid. However, "old" icing will take longer to dry. Make fresh royal icing for any detail work.

■ Gingerbread Dough
[Makes enough for 1 house]

For best results, bake gingerbread on a day when the humidity is low.

Materials

6 cups flour	2 eggs
1 teaspoon ginger	shortening to grease cookie sheets
1 teaspoon ground cloves	2 large mixing bowls
1-1/2 teaspoons ground nutmeg	mixing spoon
1 tablespoon cinnamon	floured surface for kneading
3/4 teaspoon salt	cookie sheets
1 teaspoon baking soda	rolling pin
1/2 cup butter at room temperature	sharp knife
1/2 cup shortening	paper towels
1 cup sugar	refrigerator
1-1/4 cup molasses	oven

Procedure

1. Combine 5 cups of flour with the spices, salt, and baking soda in a mixing bowl.

2. Mix the shortening and butter in other mixing bowl. Cream in the sugar.

3. Add the molasses and eggs.

4. Slowly add the dry ingredients.

5. Scoop the dough out of the bowl and place it on a lightly floured kneading surface. Knead, adding more flour if necessary, to make a substantial dough.

6. Let the dough mellow for 1 hour, so that it rolls out well. Refrigerate for the last 1/2 hour.

7. Grease the cookie sheets with shortening.

8. Preheat the oven to 300°.

9. While the oven is preheating or earlier, cut patterns from waxed paper in the shapes of the sides and roof of the house. (See "Gingerbread House Templates," p. 135.)

10. Place the dough on the cookie sheet and roll it out with the rolling pin. The dough should be 1/4-inch thick. Lay the waxed paper templates over the rolled-out dough and cut the pieces with a sharp knife.

11. Remove the waxed paper.

12. Bake thin gingerbread for 6 minutes. Thicker gingerbread may need to bake between 10 and 15 minutes.

13. Place large pieces of gingerbread on paper towels to dry out overnight.

14. Any dough not baked can be wrapped and stored in the refrigerator. Remove it from the refrigerator 30 minutes before rolling and baking.

Constructing the Gingerbread House

1. Create a rigid base for the house. Metal trays, pizza circles, and plastic platters work well.

2. Cut a piece of waxed paper, 7 by 7-1/2 inches, to mark the floor. Attach it to the base with a bit of royal icing.

3. Apply royal icing along the bottom edge of the gingerbread house front.

4. Align the house front with the front edge of the waxed-paper floor and place it on the base. It may need to be propped temporarily.

5. Apply royal icing along the bottom edge of one side of the house.

6. Align the house side with the side edge of the waxed-paper floor and place it on the base. Using icing, attach the house side to the house front.

7. Apply royal icing along the bottom edge of the house back.

8. Align the house back with the back edge of the waxed-paper floor and place it on the base. Using icing, attach the house back and the side together.

9. Apply royal icing along the bottom edge of the other house side.

10. Align the house side with the side edge of the waxed-paper floor and place it on the base. Using icing, attach the side to the house front. Then attach the side to the house back.

11. Let the house frame set for at least 1 hour.

12. Apply royal icing to the top edges of all 4 pieces of the gingerbread frame.

13. Place the roof pieces on the frame pieces. Using icing, join the two roof pieces.

14. Let the entire gingerbread house dry for at least 1 hour before decorating.

15. Now comes the best part—decorating. Following are some gingerbread house decorating ideas:

    Inverted ice cream cones with pointed ends make nice pine trees.

    Small pretzels become excellent fencing.

    Vanilla wafers make great roof shingles.

    Pretzel rods can become chimneys or even the walls of log cabins.

    Animal crackers can provide some interesting gingerbread pets.

    Pieces of licorice whip can divide sections of walls into bricks.

    Tinted coconut simulates grass.

    Granola can become gravel.

    Colored sugars make everything glitter.

    Marshmallows can become smoke puffs from a chimney.

■ Easy Gingerbread Houses
[Makes 1 house]

Easy gingerbread houses may not be as elaborate as those made from scratch. However, they take less time and are particularly successful with younger students.

Materials

6 double graham crackers
small, serrated knife
"Royal Icing" (see p. 135)
decorating materials

base such as metal tray, pizza
  circle, or plastic platter
props such as bottles of glue or
  containers of paint

Procedure

1. Two of the double graham crackers will be front and back walls; two will be the sides; two will be the roof. To make peaks at the tops of the walls, cut with the knife using a "sawing" motion.

2. Spread the bottom edge of the front wall with royal icing and attach to the base. Prop with bottles of glue until the icing sets.

3. Spread royal icing on the sides and bottom of a side wall (one long edge, two short edges). Attach the side wall to the front wall and to the base. Prop with bottles of glue until icing sets.

4. Spread the side and bottom edges of the back wall with royal icing and attach to the base and the standing side. Prop with bottles of glue until icing sets.

5. Spread the other side wall graham cracker with royal icing on the two side and bottom edges. Attach to the base, front wall, and back wall. Prop with bottles of glue until icing sets.

6. Allow to set and remove any props.

7. The last two double crackers will form the roof. Join the two crackers' long sides together with royal icing.

8. Apply royal icing to the top edges of the front and back walls.

9. Place the roof crackers on the wall crackers with the roof crackers forming a peak. Let set.

10. Decorate and display.

20
Dairy Products

Making butter, cheese, and other dairy products is an excellent hands-on project for students. Because these foods date back thousands of years, they relate well to units on ancient civilizations as well as the American Colonial period. These projects also can promote healthy eating habits by relating a basic food—milk—to the processes of science.

All containers and utensils used to make milk products must be exceptionally clean.

■ Sweet Butter
[Makes about 1 cup]

Instead of using the electric mixer (below), make this a group project in the following way: Pour the cream into a jar. Add one extremely clean marble. Screw on the jar lid. Have each student shake the jar for a few moments and then pass it on. The shaking gets harder after a while.

Materials

1 pint heavy cream
bowl
electric mixer

strainer
salt (optional)

Procedure

1. Pour the heavy cream into a bowl. Start to beat with the mixer.
2. Keep beating after it becomes whipped cream.
3. Soon it will get thicker. Lumps of butter will form.
4. Strain the mixture. The liquid is buttermilk. Add salt to the butter if desired.

■ Cinnamon-Raisin Butter
[Makes about 3/4 cup]

Top Irish soda bread (see p. 123) with this easy-to-make butter.

Materials

1/2 cup softened butter
1 teaspoon ground cinnamon
3 tablespoons powdered sugar

1/4 cup raisins
mixing bowl
mixing spoon

Procedure

1. Beat together the cinnamon, powdered sugar, and raisins until the mixture is fluffy. Gently mix in the raisins.

■ Maple-Nut Butter
[Makes about 3/4 cup]

Lavish this butter on hot corn bread (see p. 119). The corn bread soaks up the butter immediately.

Materials
1/2 cup softened butter	mixing bowl
1/4 cup maple syrup	mixing spoon
1 tablespoon chopped pecans	

Procedure
1. Beat ingredients together until smooth.

■ Honey Butter
[Makes about 3/4 cup]

Honey butter and biscuits (see p. 125) make a tasty combination.

Materials
1/2 cup softened butter	mixing bowl
1/4 cup honey	mixing spoon

Procedure
1. Beat ingredients together until fluffy.

■ Orange Butter
[Makes about 1/2 cup]

For a tasty treat, spread orange butter on orange-honey bread (see p. 124).

Materials
1/2 cup softened butter	mixing bowl
1-1/2 teaspoons grated orange peel	mixing spoon
3 tablespoons powdered sugar	

Procedure
1. Beat ingredients together until smooth.

■ Ice Cream Without the Ice Cream Maker
[Makes 2-3/4 cups—enough for 6 students]

This ice cream requires no expensive machinery. Many students can participate in the process.

Materials

1 rennet tablet (available through chemical supply houses or at grocery stores in the pudding section under the name *junket*)
1 tablespoon cold water
1/3 cup sugar
1-1/2 cups milk
1 cup heavy cream
2 teaspoons vanilla

small bowl
stainless steel pot
mixing spoon
freezer-safe container
large fork
electric mixer
stove or heating element
refrigerator

Procedure

1. In the small bowl, dissolve the rennet tablet in the cold water.
2. Combine the sugar, milk, and heavy cream in the stainless steel pot. Heat, stirring constantly, until the mixture is lukewarm.
3. Add the vanilla.
4. Add the rennet.
5. Pour the mixture into the freezer-proof container and let stand 15 minutes.
6. Place the container in the freezer until the mixture is fairly frozen but not completely hard.
7. Remove the container from the freezer. Using the fork, break the mixture into large pieces.
8. Whip the mixture with the electric mixer for 3 minutes.
9. Place the mixture back in the freezer until completely frozen.

■ Curds and Whey
[Makes 1 quart]

Water comprises about 88 percent of milk's content. The remaining 12 percent is composed of milk solids—a combination of caseins (proteins), milk sugar, milk fats, vitamins, and minerals. Curds and whey result when vinegar is added to milk. The vinegar curdles the caseins, producing the curds. The resulting liquid is the whey. Students can pretend to be Little Miss Muffet, but they should not eat the curds and whey like she did. However, cottage cheese (see below), made from curds and whey, is palatable.

Materials

1 quart whole milk	container
1/2 cup vinegar	spoon

Procedure

1. Pour the milk into the container. Add the vinegar and stir.

2. Let the mixture sit for 2 to 3 minutes. The milk will separate into the curds (the solid part) and the whey (the liquid part).

■ Cottage Cheese
[Makes 1 cup]

Start draining the curds early in the day so that the cottage cheese can be eaten the same day.

Materials

curds from "Curds and Whey" (see above)	colander cheesecloth

Procedure

1. Line the colander with cheesecloth. Pour the curds into the cheesecloth.

2. Cover with another piece of cheesecloth. Let it drain for 6 hours.

3. Cut it into smaller pieces and eat.

■ Yogurt
[Makes 1/2 gallon—enough for 12 students]

This plain yogurt has a tart, tangy taste. Students enjoy watching a little bit of yogurt become 1/2 gallon!

Materials

1/2 gallon milk
small container (1 cup) of plain yogurt, without additives or preservatives
large stainless steel pot with lid
hot tap water
spoon

small, extremely clean containers with lids
large towel
fruit (optional)
stove or heating element
refrigerator

Procedure

1. Heat the milk over medium heat in the stainless steel pot until the milk almost boils. Simmer for 15 minutes. This will kill any bacteria. Cool until lukewarm.
2. Stir in the yogurt. Pour the yogurt mixture into the containers and put on the lids.
3. Clean the pot. Put the containers of yogurt into the pot.
4. Fill the pot nearly up to the lids of the containers with hot tap water. Place the lid on the pot. Wrap the towel around the pot.
5. Let stand for 5 hours. Open one container. The contents should be thickened to the consistency of yogurt.
6. Refrigerate all the containers. Add fruit if desired at serving time.

■ Yogurt Cheese
[Makes 1 cup]

Yogurt cheese resembles cream cheese. It can be used to make dips.

Materials

3 cups plain yogurt
colander

cheesecloth
container with lid

Procedure

1. Place the colander in the sink and line with the cheesecloth.
2. Empty the yogurt into the cheesecloth.
3. Allow the yogurt to drain until the next day.
4. Refrigerate the yogurt in the container with lid.

■ Frozen Yogurt Treats
[Makes 4-3/4 cups—enough for 10 students]

Strawberries and bananas make a good fruit combination. So do blueberries and peaches.

Materials

2 cups fresh fruit
1/4 cup juice concentrate
2-1/2 cups plain yogurt
2 teaspoons vanilla

blender
10 paper cups
craft sticks

Procedure

1. Puree the fruits and juice in the blender.
2. Mix in the yogurt and vanilla.
3. Pour into the paper cups. Place in the freezer.
4. When the mixture is fairly stiff, add the craft sticks to serve as handles.
5. Peel off the paper cups at serving time.

■ Cream Cheese
[Makes 1 cup]

Flavored cream cheese spreads have become quite popular. Stir in raisins and a bit of cinnamon.

Materials

3 cups heavy cream
4 tablespoons buttermilk
mixing bowl
mixing spoon

colander
cheesecloth
spatter screen

Procedure

1. Combine the heavy cream and the buttermilk in the mixing bowl.
2. Line the colander with the cheesecloth and place in the sink.
3. Pour the mixture into the cheesecloth.
4. Wash and dry the mixing bowl.
5. Place the spatter screen over the mixing bowl.
6. Place the cheesecloth on the screen so that the liquid will drain into the bowl.
7. Leave for at least a day. The longer the cheese stands, the drier it will be.

■ Hard Cheese
[Makes about 2 pounds]

This basic recipe makes a cheese somewhat like a Colby. It can be modified by changing the type of milk, varying the cooking time, or introducing cultures other than buttermilk. However, this recipe allows students to be part of all the steps. The actual cheese making takes only a day. Pressing the cheese adds another 5 days. The cheese needs to mellow for 1 month before it can be consumed.

Materials

1 gallon pasteurized milk
1 cup cultured buttermilk
1/8 rennet tablet (available through chemical supply houses) or 1-1/4 junket tablets (available at grocery stores in the puddings section)
1/4 cup cool water
3 tablespoons coarse, non-iodized salt
small amount of vegetable oil
2 stainless steel pans, 1 large enough to contain the gallon of milk but small enough to fit inside the other pan (together the pans act as a double boiler)

small bowl
small mixing spoon
knife
candy thermometer
large mixing spoon
cheesecloth
colander
cheese press (see p. 147)

Procedure

1. Place the smaller stainless steel pan inside the larger one. Add the milk to the smaller one.

2. Fill the larger pan with water until the water level is equal to the milk level.

3. Heat the milk to 88° and add the cultured buttermilk.

4. Allow the mixture to rest for at least 1/2 hour but up to 3 hours. The longer it rests, the sharper the cheese will be.

5. Place the rennet tablet or junket tablet in the small bowl. Add the water and dissolve.

6. Pour the rennet mixture into the milk mixture and stir. Let sit for several hours until the milk has coagulated.

7. Using the knife, cut the curd into very small pieces.

8. Knead the curd for 10 minutes, until the whey separates.

9. Gradually heat until the curds (still inside the double boiler) reach 102°. Keep at 102° for 1 hour. Stir frequently.

10. Line the colander with the cheesecloth. Pour in the curds. Strain the whey away.

11. Slowly stir in the salt.

12. Remove the curd-filled cheesecloth from the colander and tie a knot in the cheesecloth.
13. Place the wrapped curds in the cheese press. Apply a bit of pressure with 1 brick for 1 hour.
14. Increase the pressure by using both bricks. Press for 5 hours.
15. Remove the cheese from the press. Let it dry in a cool, well-ventilated area for 5 days.
16. Coat the cheese with the vegetable oil. This will prevent molding. Return the cheese to a cool, well-ventilated area. Let the cheese ripen for 1 month.

■ Cheese Press

This homemade cheese press has two purposes. It gives the cheese a shape, and it forces liquids out of the developing cheese.

Materials

2 bricks
2 plastic bags
dinner plate

spatter shield
springform pan with bottom

Procedure

1. Place a brick into each plastic bag and secure. These will be the weights.
2. Invert the dinner plate and place it on the bottom of the sink.
3. Place the spatter shield on top of the plate.
4. Open the springform pan and remove the bottom. Do not secure the clamp on the side of the springform pan.
5. Place the pan on top of the spatter shield.
6. The wrapped cheese should go inside the springform pan.
7. Place the pan bottom on top of the cheese.
8. Align the bricks on top of the pan bottom. The pan bottom will distribute the weight of the bricks.

21

Treats That Students Can Make

■ Basic Cookies
[Makes 6 dozen]

Few things can beat the smell and taste of freshly baked cookies. This recipe can be adapted in many ways. The dough can even be rolled out and shaped with cookie cutters. One group of students that I know bakes heart-shaped cookies around Valentine's Day. At lunch they sell the cookies to schoolmates. The proceeds go to the American Heart Association.

Materials

1 teaspoon baking powder	shortening to grease cookie sheets
3/4 teaspoon salt	medium-size mixing bowl
1/4 teaspoon baking soda	large mixing bowl
3-3/4 cups flour	mixing spoon
3/4 cup butter	waxed paper
2/3 cup shortening	knife
1 cup brown sugar	cookie sheets
1/2 cup sugar	refrigerator
2 eggs	oven
2-1/2 teaspoons vanilla	

Procedure

1. Combine the baking powder, salt, baking soda, and flour in the medium-size mixing bowl.
2. In the large mixing bowl, blend the butter and shortening. Slowly add the sugars, eggs, and vanilla.
3. Mixing continuously, add the dry ingredients to the shortening-sugar mixture.
4. Divide the dough into thirds. Shape each portion into a log. Wrap each log in waxed paper and refrigerate overnight. Or, the dough can be frozen for later use.
5. Remove the dough from the refrigerator. Take off the waxed paper. Cut the dough into 1/2-inch thick slices.
6. Lightly grease the cookie sheets with shortening.
7. Place the cookies on the cookie sheets.
8. Bake at 400° for 6 minutes.

■ Chocolate Chip Cookies
[Makes 6 dozen]

Using the "Basic Cookies" recipe (above), add 1-1/2 cups semisweet chocolate chips to the shortening-sugar mixture before adding the flour.

■ Chocolate Cookies
[Makes 6 dozen]

Use the "Basic Cookies" recipe (see p. 149). In a microwave oven, melt 4 ounces of unsweetened chocolate and add to the shortening-sugar mixture before stirring in the flour.

■ Sugar Cookies
[Makes 6 dozen]

Use the "Basic Cookies" recipe (see p. 149). Sprinkle colored sugar on the cookies before baking.

■ Snickerdoodles
[Makes 6 dozen]

Snickerdoodles are drop cookies. They require less work and time than sliced cookies.

Procedure
1. Follow the "Basic Cookies" recipe (see p. 149). Do not slice the cookies but drop the dough by spoonfuls onto the cookie sheets.
2. Combine 1/3 cup sugar with 2 tablespoons cinnamon. Sprinkle on the cookies before baking.

■ Butterscotch Cookies
[Makes 6 dozen]

Follow the "Basic Cookies" recipe (see p. 149). However, replace the cup of sugar with another cup of brown sugar.

■ Fortune Cookies
[Makes 30 cookies]

Fortune cookies probably did not originate in China. However, these cookies make a great treat on the Chinese New Year. Bake 4 cookies at a time. When they come out of the oven, they are flexible enough to fold. After sitting for a few minutes, they harden and will break rather than fold. If they do harden before they can be bent, return them to the oven for 20 seconds.

Materials

1 cup flour	large mixing bowl
2 tablespoons cornstarch	mixing spoon
1/2 cup sugar	electric mixer
1/2 cup vegetable oil	cookie sheets
4 egg whites (1/2 cup)	spatula
2 teaspoons grated orange rind	30 fortunes, typed on slips of paper
1 tablespoon orange flavoring	paper cups
shortening to grease cookie sheets	oven

Procedure

1. In the large bowl combine the flour, cornstarch, and sugar.
2. Add the oil and egg whites. Beat at high speed until the batter is well blended.
3. Add the grated orange rind and orange flavoring.
4. Grease the cookie sheets. Drop level tablespoons of batter onto the cookie sheets.
5. Use the spatula to spread the batter into a 4-inch-diameter circle. Bake 4 cookies at a time.
6. Bake at 325° for 10 minutes, or until cookies are lightly browned.
7. Remove the cookies with a spatula.
8. Place a fortune in the center of a cookie. Fold the cookie in half.
9. Fold the cookie in half again by creasing the folded edge on the edge of the mixing bowl.
10. To make sure the cookie retains its shape, place the cookie in a paper cup with the points down. Let the cookies harden for 2 minutes. Remove them from the cups.
11. Repeat with the rest of the cookies. Bake the rest of the batter.
12. Store cookies in an airtight container.

■ Chocolate Crisp Cookies
[Makes 3 dozen]

Because chocolate crisp cookies require no baking, they are quick and easy to make. Students can do just about all the steps.

Materials

8-ounce milk chocolate bar	mixing spoon
1/3 cup shredded coconut	aluminum foil
2 cups crisp rice cereal	refrigerator
microwave-safe bowl	microwave oven

Procedure

1. Microwave the chocolate at medium setting for 1 minute.
2. Add the coconut and crisp rice cereal.
3. Drop by spoonfuls onto aluminum foil.
4. Refrigerate for 1 hour.

■ Chocolate and Peanut Butter Treats
[Makes 15 treats]

These no-bake treats are sweet, salty, and crunchy, all at the same time.

Materials

1 package (6 ounces) semisweet chocolate chips	microwave-safe bowl
2/3 cup chunky peanut butter	mixing spoon
1 container (3 ounces) chow mein noodles	aluminum foil
	microwave oven

Procedure

1. Combine the peanut butter and chocolate chips in the microwave-safe bowl.
2. Microwave at high setting for 3 minutes or until melted.
3. Add the noodles and stir.
4. Drop by spoonfuls onto aluminum foil and let cool.

■ Gorp

[Makes 3 cups—enough for 6 students]

This makes a good mid-morning school snack. Gorp is also great for carrying on hikes.

Materials

1 cup raisins
1 cup M&M® candies
1/2 cup salted peanuts

1/2 cup unsalted peanuts
bowl
small bags

Procedure

1. Mix the ingredients together and put into small bags.

■ Peanut Brittle

[Makes 3 cups—enough for 6 students]

Peanut brittle stores well for a long time. The peanuts add some nutrition to this candy.

Materials

3 tablespoons butter
1 cup shelled peanuts
3 cups sugar
dinner plate
aluminum foil

saucepan
mixing spoon
hot pads
stove or heating element

Procedure

1. Cover the dinner plate with aluminum foil. Generously grease the foil with butter.
2. Distribute the peanuts evenly around the plates.
3. Heat the sugar in the saucepan at high heat. When the sugar begins to melt, turn down the heat and stir continuously.
4. When the sugar is all melted, remove the pan from the heat with hot pads. Pour the melted sugar over the peanuts.
5. Let cool. Peel the candy from the aluminum foil and break into pieces.

■ Caramel Corn
[Makes 2-1/2 quarts]

Melting the caramels in the microwave makes this recipe fun.

Materials

28 unwrapped caramels	large mixing bowl
2 tablespoons cold water	cookie sheet
2-1/2 quarts popped popcorn	shortening
microwave-safe bowl	microwave oven
mixing spoon	oven

Procedure

1. Place the caramels and water together in the microwave-safe bowl.
2. Microwave the caramels and water at high setting for 1-1/2 minutes.
3. Stir. If the caramels are not melted, microwave at high setting for 30 seconds.
4. Stir again. Repeat step 3 until the caramels are melted.
5. Place the popcorn into the large mixing bowl. Pour the sauce over the popcorn and stir until the popcorn is coated.
6. Grease the cookie sheet.
7. Pour the popcorn-caramel mixture onto the greased cookie sheet.
8. Spread the mixture out.
9. Bake at 250° for 20 minutes. Break into pieces.

■ Cheese Popcorn
[Makes 2 quarts]

Plain popcorn is very nutritious. The cheese adds extra food value and lots of panache.

Materials

1/4 cup butter or margarine, melted	small bowl
1/2 cup grated Parmesan cheese	large bowl
2 quarts popped popcorn	mixing spoon

Procedure

1. Mix the butter and cheese in the small bowl.
2. Put the popcorn into the large bowl.
3. Pour the butter-cheese mixture over the popcorn. Stir to distribute the mixture.

■ Crisp Rice Treats
[Makes 15 treats]

Recipes for crisp rice cereal treats have been around for a long time. This recipe uses the microwave oven to speed the process. The recipe can be modified by adding 1/4 cup peanut butter to the marshmallow-margarine mixture. Raisins, dried fruit, or chocolate chips can be added before the mixture is placed in the pan.

Materials:

1 package (10 ounces) marshmallows	mixing spoon
or 4 cups miniature marshmallows	microwave-safe bowl
1/4 cup margarine or butter	13-by-9-by-2-inch pan
6 cups crisp rice cereal	spatula
vegetable oil cooking spray	microwave oven

Procedure

1. Microwave the margarine or butter and marshmallows at high setting for 2 minutes.
2. Stir and microwave at high setting for 1 minute.
3. Add the cereal and stir until the cereal is coated.
4. Coat the pan and spatula with vegetable oil cooking spray.
5. Pour the cereal-marshmallow mixture into the pan.
6. Distribute the mixture evenly around the pan with the coated spatula.
7. Cool and cut into squares.

■ Peanut Butter
[Makes 2 cups]

Homemade peanut butter may separate after a while. Simply stir it to blend the oil back in. Store in the refrigerator.

Materials

3 cups shelled, roasted peanuts	blender
small amount of vegetable oil	

Procedure

1. Put the peanuts into the blender and chop until smooth.
2. Add a bit of oil if necessary to increase smoothness.

■ Cereal Snacks
[Makes 9 cups]

The peanut butter and cereal make this snack somewhat nutritious. It stores well.

Materials

3/4 cup semisweet chocolate chips
1/2 cup peanut butter
1/2 cup margarine
1/2 teaspoon vanilla
9 cups non-flake cereal
   (e.g., Corn Chex®)
1-1/2 cups powdered sugar

microwave-safe bowl
large bowl
spoon
gallon-size plastic bag
waxed paper
small sandwich bags
microwave oven

Procedure

1. In the microwave-safe bowl, combine the chocolate chips, peanut butter, and margarine.
2. Microwave at high setting for 1 minute. Stir.
3. Add the vanilla.
4. Pour the cereal into the large bowl.
5. Pour the margarine mixture over the cereal, stirring to coat the pieces.
6. Pour the mixture into the plastic bag. Add the powdered sugar. Close the bag.
7. Shake the bag until the cereal is well coated.
8. Pour the cereal snacks onto waxed paper and let cool.
9. Place the mixture in small sandwich bags and distribute to the students.

■ Marshmallow Delights
[Makes 40]

Not many snacks are this easy to make. Students can set up an assembly line of "dippers" and "toppers."

Materials

10-ounce package marshmallows
12-ounce package semisweet
   chocolate chips
small containers of coconut,
   sprinkles, and chopped nuts

large, flat pan
microwave-safe bowl
fork
microwave oven
freezer and refrigerator

Procedure

1. Lay the marshmallows on the large, flat pan.
2. Place in the freezer for 15 minutes.
3. Microwave the chocolate chips until melted.
4. Using the fork, dip the frozen marshmallows into the melted chocolate.
5. Then roll the marshmallows in the toppings.
6. Chill and eat.

■ Pizza Muffins
[Each English muffin half makes an individual pizza]

These quick and filling pizza muffins are a great finish to a unit on nutrition. Each muffin uses all four basic food groups.

Materials

English muffins, split
pizza sauce
grated mozzarella cheese
diced green peppers, mushrooms,
   olives, onions, pepperoni

spoon
cookie sheet
oven broiler or toaster oven

Procedure

1. Spread a spoonful of pizza sauce onto each English muffin half.
2. Sprinkle on the cheese.
3. Add the toppings to taste.
4. Place the muffins on the cookie sheet and broil in the oven until the cheese melts.

■ Latkes
[Makes 15 latkes]

These are Jewish potato pancakes. They are delicious served alone or topped with applesauce or sour cream.

Materials

5 large potatoes
1 small onion
2 eggs
1/2 teaspoon salt
3/4 cup flour
1/2 teaspoon baking powder
shortening to grease electric
   frying pan
waxed paper
potato peeler

grater
mixing bowl
mixing spoon
electric frying pan
spatula
applesauce or sour cream or
   both (optional)
serving plate
cutting board

Procedure

1. Cover a small work area with waxed paper.
2. Peel the potatoes and discard the peels.
3. Beat the eggs in the mixing bowl.
4. Grate the potatoes onto the cutting board and add them to the mixing bowl.
5. Chop the onion on the cutting board and add to the mixing bowl.
6. Add the salt, flour, and baking powder.
7. Heat the electric frying pan to a high temperature. Grease.
8. Drop spoonfuls of the potato mixture into the frying pan. Let brown. Turn with the spatula and let brown on the other side.
9. Place browned latkes on the serving plate and continue to prepare the rest of the latkes.
10. Serve with applesauce or sour cream if desired.

■ Toasted Pumpkin Seeds
[Makes 2 cups]

Students can save their seeds when they carve their Halloween pumpkins. Keep the toasted seeds until Thanksgiving and add them to a feast.

Materials

2 cups unhulled pumpkin seeds, cleaned and washed	shortening cookie sheet
4 teaspoons salt	colander
water	extra salt (optional)
bowl	oven

Procedure

1. Pour the seeds into the bowl and cover with water.
2. Stir in the 4 teaspoons of salt. Soak the seeds for 4 hours.
3. Generously coat the cookie sheet with shortening.
4. Drain the seeds in the colander and spread them on the cookie sheet.
5. Shake on additional salt, if desired.
6. Toast in a 300° oven until the seeds are amber brown (10 to 15 minutes).

■ Apple Butter
[Makes approximately 1 cup]

Apple butter was a Colonial favorite. It takes quite a while to make, but it is worth the effort.

Materials

1 large can or jar applesauce	pan
cinnamon or cloves or both	spoon
butter	

Procedure

1. Cook the applesauce on low heat. Stir often.
2. Add the spices to taste.
3. Soon the applesauce should become dark and thick.
4. Add 1 pat of butter for each cup of applesauce.
5. Cool and spread over bread.
6. Refrigerate any apple butter not eaten.

■ Fruit Leather
[Makes enough for 1 class]

Pioneers preserved their fall fruit harvest by making fruit leather. Today's pre-packaged fruit-roll snacks are a modern version of fruit leather.

Materials

4 quarts fruit (such as apples, peaches, or apricots), peeled, cored, and cut	blender
	large pot
	cookie sheets
1 to 2 cups apple juice	freezer paper
honey	cheesecloth
cinnamon	cake rack
cornstarch	stove or heating element

Procedure

1. Puree the fruit in the blender.
2. Pour the fruit into the large pot and add the apple juice.
3. Over low heat, bring the mixture to a boil.
4. Add the honey and cinnamon according to taste.
5. Reduce the temperature until the mixture is just simmering. Simmer the mixture, stirring often, until it has the consistency of apple butter.
6. Cover the cookie sheets with freezer paper.
7. Pour the mixture onto the cookie sheets so that the mixture forms a layer 1/4-inch thick.
8. Cover with cheesecloth and place in the sun or a warm area to dry. Drying may take up to 10 days.
9. Fruit leather can also be dried in a low-temperature oven or food drier.
10. When the fruit leather is dried enough to keep its shape, cut it into strips. Place the strips on the cake rack to make sure all sides dry.
11. Dry until the surface of the fruit leather no longer feels sticky. Sprinkle cornstarch on the strips and remove from the cake rack. The cornstarch keeps the pieces from clinging to one another.
12. Store in freezer paper.

■ Oven-Dried Fruit and Raisins
[Makes about half as much dried fruit as the initial amount of fresh fruit]

Colonists dried apples by coring, slicing, and stringing them. The strings were placed near the fireplace to hasten the drying.

Materials

fresh fruit (see directions for preparation below)

cookie sheet
plastic bag

Procedure

1. Prepare fruit:

   Preparing Grapes (Raisins)
   a. Wash white seedless grapes.
   b. Place them in boiling water until the skins split.
   c. Drain.

   Preparing Apples and Peaches
   a. Wash the fruit.
   b. For peaches, peel and remove the pits. For apples, peel and core.
   c. Cut into thin slices and follow above directions for dried fruit.

   Preparing Berries and Cherries
   a. Remove cherry pits.
   b. Wash, drain, and follow above directions for dried fruit

2. Place the fruit on the cookie sheet.

3. Place the sheet in an oven at 150°. Bake for 6 hours, or until the fruit is dry but not brittle.

4. Cool and store in the plastic bag.

■ Sun-Dried Fruit and Raisins
[Makes about half as much dried fruit as the initial amount of fresh fruit]

Remember to bring the fruit indoors each night. If the fruit is left out at night, the evening dew will plump up the fruit again.

Materials

fresh fruit (see directions for preparation of "Oven-Dried Fruit and Raisins," p. 161)

cheesecloth or netting
plastic bag
large, flat pan

Procedure

1. Prepare fruit and place in the pan.
2. Cover the pan with netting or cheesecloth to keep out bugs and birds.
3. Place the pan in the sun. Turn the fruit several times so that it will dry evenly.
4. At the end of the day, bring the pan back in.
5. The next day, put the pan back out in the sunshine.
6. Depending on the temperature and humidity, the grapes should become raisins in 2 or 3 days. Larger pieces of fruit may take up to 5 days to dry.
7. Store the fruit in a plastic bag and place in the refrigerator.

■ Berry Water Ice
[Makes 1-1/2 quarts]

"Nutritious and still delicious," is what students will say.

Materials

3 cups fruit (strawberries, blueberries, cranberries)
1-1/2 cups sugar
3 cups water
pot

blender
spoon
freezer-safe container
stove or heating element

Procedure

1. Simmer the fruit and sugar in the water until the berries are soft.
2. Puree in the blender.
3. Pour into the freezer-safe container and place in the freezer.
4. Stir several times while the mixture is freezing.

■ Lemon Water Ice
[Makes 1-1/2 quarts]

Water ice is becoming very popular. It is easy to make and quite refreshing.

Materials

4 cups water
1-1/2 cups sugar
1 cup lemon juice
pot

spoon
freezer-safe container
stove or heating element

Procedure

1. Boil the water and sugar together for 3 minutes. Cool.
2. Add the lemon juice.
3. Pour the mixture into the freezer-safe container and place in the freezer.
4. Stir several times while the mixture is freezing.

■ Frozen Fruit Treats
[Makes 6 treats]

These treats are very nutritious. They also help students understand how water can take different forms.

Materials

1 small package strawberry- or
    raspberry-flavored gelatin
1/2 cup boiling water
1/2 tablespoon lemon juice
20-ounce can pineapple chunks
    with juice
2 bananas
mixing bowl

mixing spoon
blender
knife
paper cups or small plastic
    containers
craft sticks
freezer

Procedure

1. Mix the gelatin and boiling water in the mixing bowl.
2. Pour into the blender. Add the lemon juice and the can of pineapple.
3. Cut the bananas into small pieces and add.
4. Blend until pureed. Pour into the paper cups and place in the freezer.
5. When almost solid, insert the craft sticks. Return to the freezer until solid.

22
Miscellaneous

■ Applesauce-Cinnamon Decorations

Use holiday cookie cutters to make decorations to hang on a tree. Use heart-shaped cookie cutters to make Valentine's Day gifts. Make sure the recipients of these gifts know the decorations are not edible.

Materials

1 cup applesauce	rolling pin
4.12-ounce container of ground cinnamon	cookie cutters
	straw
mixing bowl	drying rack
mixing spoon	spatula
waxed paper	ribbon

Procedure

1. Mix the applesauce into the cinnamon until a stiff dough forms.
2. Pour the mixture onto the waxed paper. Roll to 1/4-inch thickness.
3. Cut into shapes or use cookie cutters. Using the straw, make a hole for a ribbon.
4. Lay the decorations on a rack.
5. Flip them over twice a day for 10 days so that the edges will not curl.
6. When the decorations are thoroughly dry, thread a ribbon through the hole on each one and knot it.

■ Deckled Paper

Another way to age paper is to deckle the edge. The paper's edge will look frayed, typical of old paper.

Materials

paper	ruler
sponge	water

Procedure

1. Slightly dampen the edges of the paper with the sponge.
2. Place the ruler on the paper, parallel to and near the paper's edge.
3. Hold the ruler down firmly with one hand and tear the paper against the ruler with the other hand.
4. Let the paper dry.

■ Aged Paper

This process makes new paper look old. Students can use the technique to age newly created diary entries, letters, and maps.

Materials

diary entry, letter, or map

large bowl

2 cups fairly hot coffee or tea

newspaper

Procedure

1. Pour the hot coffee or tea into the bowl.

2. Crumple the diary entry, letter, or map.

3. Submerge the paper in the liquid.

4. Let stand until cool.

5. Remove from the liquid and dry on the newspaper.

■ Spatter Painting

Smocks are a good idea for this project. Students like to watch the randomness of the spatters.

Materials

newspaper

toothbrush

piece of window screening

paints

blank paper

4 small blocks of boxes
(1-1/2 to 2 inches tall) to
form props for the screen

Procedure

1. Cover the work area with newspaper.

2. Place the blank paper on the newspaper.

3. Place a block or box at each corner of the paper.

4. Place the window screening above the paper on the blocks.

5. Load the toothbrush with paint.

6. Brush the toothbrush across the screening. Paint will spatter over the paper.

7. To make a negative print, cut out a shape such as a heart. Place the heart on the blank paper. Spatter the paper and carefully remove the shape. The spatter paint will outline the shape.

■ Pumpkin Pie Spice Decorations

These items make great Thanksgiving decorations and table favors. They are not edible.

Materials

3/4 cup ground cinnamon
1/4 cup ground nutmeg
1 teaspoon ground ginger
5 tablespoons white glue
3/4 cup water
mixing bowl
mixing spoon
rolling pin

extra cinnamon to dust surface
pumpkin-shaped cookie cutter
straw
waxed paper
spatula
ribbon
refrigerator

Procedure

1. Combine the cinnamon, nutmeg, ginger, and glue in the mixing bowl.
2. Add enough water to make a stiff dough.
3. Refrigerate for 3 hours.
4. Sprinkle extra cinnamon on the rolling surface and place the dough on it.
5. Knead the dough until it is pliable. Using the rolling pin, roll the dough to a 1/4-inch thickness.
6. Use the pumpkin cookie cutter to cut out the dough. With the straw, make a hole at the top of each pumpkin.
7. Place waxed paper on the work area. Lay the pumpkins on the waxed paper to dry.
8. Using the spatula, flip the pumpkins over twice a day for 1 week. This allows the pumpkins to dry evenly. They may curl if they are not turned.
9. When the pumpkins are dry, thread the holes with ribbon and hang.

■ Glue Sun Catchers

These decorations take a day or two to dry. The tricky part is removing the dried glue from the frame.

Materials

waxed paper	food coloring
cookie cutters	toothpicks
straws cut into 2-inch segments	glitter, beads, or other small
paper cups	decorations
white glue	ribbon

Procedure

1. Cover the work area with waxed paper.
2. Place the cookie cutters on the waxed paper.
3. In the paper cups, combine the white glue with the food coloring. Use toothpicks to blend colors.
4. Place a straw segment near the center top of each cookie cutter. The straw will provide a hole from which to hang the decoration.
5. Pour some of the colored glue mixture into the center of each cookie cutter. Make sure the straw is not disturbed.
6. Add glitter or other decorations if desired.
7. Allow the glue to dry. Remove the cookie cutters and waxed paper.
8. Remove or cut away the straw. String ribbon through the hole and hang.

■ Tie-dyeing

Oh, no! The '60s are back! Actually, tie-dyeing was practiced over a thousand years ago in Asia and Africa. Although students can still tie-dye T-shirts, they can also make book covers, lamp shades, scarves, and many other items. The natural dyes featured in chapter 7 can be used, but they may not be colorfast. Also, different fabrics dye at different rates. Cotton seems the most dependable. Silk dyes the quickest. Synthetic fabrics are not always predictable.

Materials

fabric
newspaper
household dye
bucket to hold dye

sink with running water
bucket of soapy water
rubber bands

Procedure

1. Wash the fabric first to eliminate any sizing.

2. Cover the work area with newspaper.

3. Prepare the dye according to manufacturer's directions. Make sure the dye is hot.

4. Dunk the fabric in the soapy water. The soap will help retain the dye.

5. Bunch the fabric at locations and tie with rubber bands. Use at least 2 rubber bands at each tie, and make sure the bands are very tight.

6. Place the fabric in the dye. The longer it remains, the darker the final color will be.

7. When the desired shade is reached, remove the fabric from the dye and rinse it in running water.

8. Remove the rubber bands to examine the pattern and hang the fabric to dry.

9. If more than one color is desired, knot and dye the fabric in one color. Let dry. Then knot and dye in another color. Always work from lighter colors to darker colors.

10. Objects such as marbles can be knotted into the fabric with rubber bands. This will create a consistently repeating pattern.

■ Batik

Batik making may be an older technique than tie-dyeing. It probably originated in eastern Asia.

Materials

newspaper	paintbrush
aluminum foil	household dye
fabric, preferably cotton	large, flat pan to hold dye
large, flat pan of cool water	sink with running water
paraffin	towels
coffee can	iron
electric frying pan	ironing board

Procedure

1. Cover the work area with newspaper.

2. Place a piece of aluminum foil on the work area.

3. Place the fabric on top of the foil. The foil will keep the paraffin-coated fabric from sticking to the newspaper.

4. Place the paraffin in the coffee can. Place the coffee can in the frying pan. Add water to the frying pan and turn on the heat. The coffee pan and frying pan act as a double boiler to help prevent the wax from catching fire.

5. When the wax has melted, dip the brush in the wax. "Paint" a picture on the fabric with the wax. Dip the brush back into the wax often. Now the fabric is a batik.

6. Place the batik in the cool water for a few minutes to harden the wax.

7. Prepare the dye according to manufacturer's directions.

8. Remove the batik from the cool water and place it in the dye. Remember that the longer the batik sits in the dye, the darker the color will be.

9. When the desired shade is reached, remove the batik from the dye. Rinse in running water.

10. Place the batik on the towel and remove excess water.

11. Heat the iron. Place the batik on the ironing board or work area. Cover the fabric with newspaper. Apply the hot iron.

12. The paraffin will melt into the newspaper and away from the batik. Change the newspaper and repeat the process until the wax is fully removed.

13. A batik crackle can be made by applying wax to the entire fabric surface. Place the batik in very cold water to chill the wax. Crumple the fabric to crack the wax. The dye enters the cracks. Dye the batik and remove the wax.

■ Marbled Paper

Marbled paper is easy to make—simply swirl some paints on top of a liquid base. and carefully place a piece of plain paper over it. Students like the "what if" possibilities of creating patterns and whirls and checking them out.

What can the students do with all the marbled paper they make? Use it to cover homemade books. Wrap a piece around an empty, clean concentrated fruit juice can for an instant pencil holder. Book marks, wrapping paper, and paper jewelry (see p. 174) are other possibilities.

Note: Never use detergent to clean the supplies. Soap of any kind can upset the next marbling session.

Materials

newspaper
baking pan, 9 by 12 inches
liquid starch
food coloring

tools such as hair picks, toothpicks,
  or paintbrushes to make patterns
blank paper
sink with running water

Procedure

1. Spread the newspaper over the work area.
2. Pour the liquid starch into the container. Make sure the starch in the pan is 1 inch deep. The liquid starch is called the size when marbling.
3. Dot food coloring onto the surface of the liquid starch.
4. Using tools, comb through the size and food coloring to make swirls and other patterns.
5. Carefully place the blank paper on the surface of the marbled starch concoction.
6. Let it rest on the surface for 30 seconds. Carefully lift it off.
7. Turn the paper over, so that the colored side is face up.
8. Let the colorings soak into the paper for 1 minute. Rinse with tap water to remove the excess coloring/starch.
9. Dry and use.

■ Shades of Gray Marbled Paper

This process gives a range of shades of gray and black. The water base makes it extremely easy to use.

Note: Never use detergent to clean the supplies. Soap of any kind can upset the next marbling session.

Materials

newspaper
baking pan, 9 by 12 inches
water
India ink

tools to make patterns
blank paper
sink with running water

Procedure

1. Spread the newspaper over the work area.
2. Pour water into the rectangular container.
3. Dot India ink on the surface of the water.
4. Using tools, make swirls and patterns out of the India ink.
5. Carefully place the blank paper on the surface of the India ink/water concoction.
6. Let it rest on the surface for 30 seconds. Lift it off carefully.
7. Turn the paper over, so that the inked side is face up.
8. Let the ink soak into the paper for 1 minute. Rinse with tap water to remove the excess ink.
9. Dry and use.

■ String Decorations

Only thin string works well for this project. Starch cannot support the weight of heavy string. Crochet thread, especially the variegated kind, produces interesting results.

Randomly wrap starch-soaked string around an inflated balloon. Let the string dry. Deflate the balloon and remove it. The result is an airy, laced spheroid.

Make small string decorations for Christmas tree ornaments or Easter eggs. Make large string decorations to liven up the walls for parties. For another project, cover only the lower portion of the balloon. When the balloon is popped and removed, the string will form a basket.

Materials

small balloon   liquid starch
medium-size bowl
crochet thread or other light string
   (15 yards for a balloon inflated to the size of a light bulb;
   30 yards for a balloon inflated to the size of a cantaloupe)

Procedure

1. Blow up the balloon to desired size and secure with a knot.
2. Pour the liquid starch into the bowl. Soak the string in the liquid starch for at least 30 minutes.
3. Remove the string from the starch and wrap it haphazardly around the balloon. Make sure all major portions of the balloon are covered.
4. Hang the balloon from a doorway or the underside of a table. Allow the starch to dry.
5. Pop and remove the balloon.

■ Paper Jewelry

Students can make necklaces from these beads in no time at all. This project nicely incorporates crafts into a study of ancient Egypt.

Materials

colorful pages from catalogs
   and magazines
scissors

glue
yarn or elastic
manufactured beads (optional)

Procedure

1. Cut the pages into isosceles triangles (2 sides should be of equal length). The base of each triangle can range from 1/2 inch to 1-1/2 inches in length. The longer the base of each triangle, the longer the resulting bead will be. The two equal sides of the triangle should be between 2 and 3 inches in length. The longer the sides, the thicker the bead will be.
2. Starting at the base edge, roll the paper to the pointed end. Leave a space in the center of the roll.
3. Glue the tip of the triangle to the rest of the rolled bead. Let dry.
4. Following steps 1 through 3, make beads of different sizes and colors.
5. String the beads on the elastic or yarn. Tie the elastic or yarn to complete the necklace or bracelet. Add other types of beads to the pattern if desired.

■ Vegetable and Fruit Stamps

An unusual still life can be created using these natural stamps. Mushrooms have particular appeal.

Materials

firm vegetables or fruits such as
   mushrooms, cauliflower,
   apples, and pears
knife

paints and paintbrushes
paper
water
paper towels

Procedure

1. Wash and dry the vegetables and fruits.
2. Cut the vegetables and fruits in half.
3. Paint the cut, flat areas with the paints.
4. Immediately stamp the vegetables and fruits on the paper surface.
5. Depending on the effect desired, the vegetables and fruits may need to be repainted every time. However, they could stamp the paper several times before needing to be repainted.

■ Potato Stamps

Potato stamps make easy the use of repeating patterns. Use stamps on large pieces of paper to make wrapping paper.

Materials

potato
knife
pencil
paints and paintbrushes

paper
water
paper towels

Procedure

1. Wash and dry the potato.
2. Cut the potato in half.
3. Draw a simple shape on the cut surface of one potato half.
4. Using the knife, cut away the potato from around the design. This leaves the design raised on the cut surface.
5. Paint the raised area with the paints.
6. Immediately stamp the potato on the paper surface.
7. Depending on the effect desired, the potato may need to be repainted every time. However, it could stamp the paper several times before needing to be repainted.

Bibliography

Bakule, Paula Dreifus, ed. *Rodale's Book of Practical Formulas: Easy-to-Make, Easy-to-Use Recipes for Hundreds of Everyday Activities and Tasks.* Emmaus, Pa.: Rodale Press, 1991.

Brown, Robert J. *333 Science Tricks & Experiments.* Blue Ridge Summit, Pa.: TAB Books, 1984.

Dennis, John V. *A Complete Guide to Bird Feeding.* New York: Alfred A. Knopf, 1994.

Deyrup, Astrith. *Tie Dyeing and Batik.* Garden City, N.Y.: Doubleday, 1974.

Hartwig, Daphne Metaxis. *Make Your Own Groceries.* New York: Bobbs-Merrill, 1979.

Hauser, Priscilla. *Create Your Own Greeting Cards and Gift Wrap with Priscilla Hauser.* Cincinnati, Ohio: North Light Books, 1994.

Hobson, Phyllis. *Making Soaps & Candles.* Pownal, Vt.: Storey Communications, 1974.

Kohl, Mary Ann. *Mudworks: Creative Clay, Dough, and Modeling Experiences.* Bellingham, Wash.: Bright Ring, 1989.

Levine, Shar. *The Paper Book and Paper Maker.* New York: Hyperion Books for Children, 1993.

Mack, Norman, ed. *Back to Basics.* Pleasantville, N.Y.: Reader's Digest Association, 1981.

Maurer, Diane Vogel, and Paul Maurer. *Marbling: A Complete Guide to Creating Beautiful Patterned Papers and Fabrics.* New York: Crescent Books, 1991.

Radke, Don. *Cheese Making at Home: The Complete Illustrated Guide.* Garden City, N.Y.: Doubleday, 1974.

Saddington, Marianne. *Making Your Own Paper.* Pownal, Vt.: Storey Communications, 1992.

Sattler, Helen Roney. *Recipes for Art and Craft Materials.* New York: Lothrop, Lee & Shepard; William Morrow, 1973.

Schneck, M. *Your Backyard Wildlife Garden*. Emmaus, Pa.: Rodale Press, 1992.

Stangel, Jean. *Crystals and Crystal Gardens You Can Grow*. New York: Franklin Watts, 1990.

———. *Magic Mixtures*. Carthage, Ill.: Fearon Teacher Aids, 1986.

Stokes, Donald, and Lillian Stokes. *The Bird Feeder Book: An Easy Guide to Attracting, Identifying, and Understanding Your Feeder Birds*. Boston: Little, Brown, 1987.

Swezey, Kenneth M., and Robert Scharff. *Formulas, Methods, Tips and Data for Home and Workshop*. New York: Harper & Row, 1979.

Terzian, Alexandra M. *The Kids' Multicultural Art Book: Art & Craft Experiences from Around the World*. Charlotte, Vt.: Williamson, 1993.

Westland, Pamela. *Candles*. Menlo Park, Calif.: Sunset, 1995.

About the Author

Diana Marks was born and raised in Colorado. Diana has been teaching for more than twenty years. She is currently employed by Council Rock School District, Bucks County, Pennsylvania, where she teaches gifted elementary children. She has also taught regular education and has worked in middle schools.

Diana resides in Washington Crossing, Pennsylvania with her husband Peter. They have two sons, Kevin and Colin. Diana loves to read and write. She also enjoys hiking and bicycling. Her volunteer activities have ranged from being a soccer coach, to hosting summer activities at the local library, to teaching bridge to senior citizens.

from # Teacher Ideas Press

ART THROUGH CHILDREN'S LITERATURE:
Creative Art Lessons for Caldecott Books
Debi Englebaugh

Help kids learn to create art with similar qualities to the award-winning illustrations of 57 Caldecott Books. ANYONE can teach art with the simple step-by-step instructions that explain a variety of principles, elements, and use of different art media.
xii, 199p. 8½x11 paper ISBN 1-56308-154-7

ART PROJECTS MADE EASY:
Recipes for Fun
Linda J. Arons

Fun, quick, and easy as pie, these art lessons are given in a simple recipe format, with vocabulary, necessary materials, step-by-step instructions, evaluation techniques, suggestions for curriculum integration, and follow-up activities. **Grades 1–6**.
xv, 165p. paper ISBN 1-56308-342-6

CULTIVATING A CHILD'S IMAGINATION THROUGH GARDENING
Nancy Allen Jurenka and Rosanne J. Blass

Each of these 45 lessons focuses on a specific book about gardening and offers related activities such as reading, writing, poetry, word play, music, dancing, dramatics, and other activities to enhance creativity and build literacy skills. **Grades K–6**.
xiv, 143p. 8½x11 paper ISBN 1-56308-452-X

THE BOOKMARK BOOK
Carolyn S. Brodie, Debra Goodrich, and Paula K. Montgomery

Count 'em! You can have 280 reproducible bookmarks that, under the guise of holding the reader's place, help teach library research skills. Covering every (well, almost) topic imaginable, they are great for awards, handouts, reminder notes—even bookmarks! **All levels**.
Cut 'n Clip Series
viii, 100p. 8½x11 paper ISBN 1-56308-300-0

CIRCUIT SENSE FOR ELEMENTARY TEACHERS AND STUDENTS:
Understanding and Building Simple Logic Circuits
Janaye Matteson Houghton and Robert S. Houghton

Your classroom will be literally buzzing, flashing, and whirring with the simple and affordable learning activities in this handbook. The kids will enjoy them almost as much as you do!
Grades K–6.
xi, 65p. 8½x11 paper ISBN 1-56308-149-0

STORYCASES:
Book Surprises to Take Home
Richard Tabor and Suzanne Ryan

Increase your students' excitement about learning by extending the process with take-home project kits designed around book themes. A great way to involve family members in the learning process, and kids love the novelty. **Grades K–2**.
xix, 161p. 8½x11 paper ISBN 1-56308-199-7

For a FREE catalog or to place an order, please contact:
Teacher Ideas Press
Dept. B13 • P.O. Box 6633 • Englewood, CO 80155-6633
1-800-237-6124, ext. 1 • Fax: 303-220-8843
E-Mail: lu-books@lu.com • www.lu.com

CREATIVE Resources